ONWARD!

For Eleanor – Your writing has added an almost lyrical element to our memoir meetings. We missed you when your overloaded schedule precluded being with us, and we are grateful to have you again in our midst. Many thanks for returning and contributing your inspiring stories. Fondly, Carolyn Young

ONWARD!

TRUE LIFE STORIES OF
CHALLENGES, CHOICES, & CHANGE

Edited by Emma Fulenwider

THE BIRREN CENTER

Cover design by Robin Brooks, www.thebeautyofbooks.com
Cover photo by Cheryl Svensson taken at Landskrona, Sweden

ISBN (Print) 978-1-7379296-0-4
ISBN (eBook) 978-1-7379296-1-1
Library of Congress Control Number: 2021920663

THE BIRREN CENTER
Laguna Woods, CA
guidedautobiography.com

Contents

PART 3 | CHANGE

Foreword

W elcome to our world! We are a community of 558 memoir teachers trained in the Guided Autobiography method of life story writing. For you to understand the powerful connection that holds us together and has been the inspiration for this collection, let me tell you about Guided Autobiography, our keystone.

The Guided Autobiography (GAB) method was created by James E. Birren, Ph.D. founding dean of the Davis School of Gerontology at the University of Southern California (USC) in the mid-1970s. Dr. Birren was an academic, a psychologist interested in research, memory, and aging but made a complete turnaround in his career path when he literally stumbled upon the power of life stories.

He was on a sabbatical, teaching the psychology of aging at the University of Hawaii, and had difficulty getting the class to engage and actively participate. In frustration, he told them all to go home and write two pages on a branching point in their lives, to bring it to class the next day, and be prepared to read it. The next day, after they had all read their stories, the class came alive. Older students were talking with younger students, making new connections with one another that lasted throughout the remainder of the term.

Dr. Birren then returned to USC and put his grad students to work researching autobiography, journaling, small groups, expressive writing, and more. From this, he created a syllabus for Guided Autobiography, a small group process to help people write their life stories two pages at a time. Guided by a facilitator with 'priming' questions based on life themes, the participants write at home, return to class, and read their stories in their small group. Reading and sharing life stories as a group is where the magic of GAB takes place. That is when people bond and really get to know one another from the inside out. It is a powerful process that boosts self-esteem, builds connections, reduces anxiety, and helps people come to terms with the life they have lived.

Jim Birren wrote three books on the GAB process, directed countless research projects on GAB beginning as early as 1980, and wrote numerous articles. In the late nineties, a group of Jim's colleagues gathered around him at UCLA. We formed the GAB workgroup and sought ways to develop and extend GAB outside of academia and into new venues. We met frequently and became best of friends. We created spinoff classes, built a website, and created a video tribute to Jim's legacy. We won the American Society on Aging award for "Most Innovative Older Adult Learning Program," and Jim and I presented GAB workshops across the nation. In 2009, I began training new GAB instructors through an online learning platform.

Jim remained active in the GAB mission until his passing in 2016 at the age of 97. We are dedicated to his legacy and his command to "Launch GAB!"

To date, the Birren Center has trained over five hundred GAB instructors worldwide. When the pandemic hit, our community of instructors worked together to offer free online GAB classes to homebound people around the world. We formed a committee to create workshops and find new ways to promote racial justice and help educate ourselves in diversity and equity. We are a supportive, connected group of memoir teachers. This is the first collection of our stories, and, as always, this is a project developed and produced by volunteers from our own membership.

We GAB memoir teachers come together with a deep and abiding belief in the power of story to heal wounds, make connections, enhance self-understanding, and promote growth. Stories connect us and bridge differences, whether racial, gender, age, ability, or religious. Once we hear another person's story, we see them more wholly and compassionately. We may not be able to walk in another person's shoes, but listening deeply to their life story is as close as it gets.

Writing, sharing, and actively listening to stories written from the heart is an act of grace. As the writer, you dig deep to uncover memories, sometimes painful, and re-examine them in a new light. You are a different person today than when the event occurred, and you can pick up the memory, hold it up to the light, and look it over closely because you now have a new perspective. For many, the tears that fall when painful memories surface is cathartic. But unless you share your story with someone, it stays locked inside of you. Once you read your story and are witnessed, you feel lighter; the energy it took to hold that memory has been released.

As you read these true stories of challenges, choices, and change, you will learn something about yourself, about humankind, and ways of being in our world. All the stories in this collection reflect a crossroads in the writer's life, sometimes chosen, often forced upon them, but one that provided new insights about the writer's personal world and our collective human experience. Our hope is that you will be inspired to pick up a pen and begin writing your own life story. Or better yet, join us in one of the many Guided Autobiography groups offered around the world.

You can find us online at www.guidedautobiography.com.

And now, Onward!

– Cheryl Svensson, Ph.D.
DIRECTOR, THE BIRREN CENTER FOR
AUTOBIOGRAPHICAL STUDIES

Introduction

This book started as a challenge posed to our global community of memoir teachers – "Tell us about a crossroads moment in your life."

As a professional writer, I approached my first Guided Autobiography class eager to impress others with my polished writing skills. But I soon found that praise was not the point. The point was something much less comfortable – personal growth.

I had always chosen the end of my story first, spotting it through a spyglass and writing my way to it. With memoir, I learned to start at the mouth of a cave and use writing as a flashlight to find my way through my past – facing the trolls I had abandoned, to gain the treasures that they guarded. When you write your way down into your soul, you come back a different person.

Memoir is medicine. Memoir heals the one who writes it. It heals the one who reads it and feels understood. It can bridge the fault-lines that crisscross our communities, dividing us by race and age and status and party.

I commend each of our authors for not only rising to the challenge, but sharing the treasures they uncovered with the rest of us. And then teaching others to do the same. I am lucky to know them, these champions of the idea that everyone has a story, and every story deserves to be saved.

These are their everyday yet extraordinary stories of standing at the crossroads of life's challenges, choices, and change. I hope their words encourage you to face your own crossroads and inspire you to write the story.

Onward!

- Emma

PART 1 | Challenges

There are some things you learn best in calm, and some in storm.

— Willa Cather

1

Beginner's Humility

by Terry Northcutt

E very year on the day after Thanksgiving, my husband and I drive to our local Annual Gingerbread House Show and Contest. It's a small affair with about thirty or forty entries. Some by experienced bakers, some by beginners. There are Victorian houses with elaborate decorative trim, there are simple houses with snow-covered roofs and windows from square pretzels, and there are whimsical structures such as the Old Woman who lived in a shoe or a replica of the Hogwarts School from the Harry Potter series.

Browsing the houses at the show a few years ago, I found myself thinking about the preschool classrooms I had visited to consult with teachers. I loved watching the children bent over blank paper, grasping primary-colored crayons in their fists and drawing skies with puffy white clouds, yellow suns, and rainbows. What I enjoyed even more was the unbridled enthusiasm and delight when a child finished their drawing and rushed to the teacher shouting, "Teacher, Teacher, look what I did!" It was the same elation I had experienced throughout my life when I had finally mastered something challenging.

These memories decided something that I had considered for many years—to be the creator of a gingerbread house instead of a spectator. At the next Gingerbread House Show, I wanted my own gingerbread house to be on display. Then, I remembered elementary school when I became aware that some classmates excelled in reading, some at athletics, and some at creative art projects. I was not one of those who excelled in art. Yet, I loved art and had always wanted to create something. And that desire, combined with my awareness of the delight of preschool children, made me think: *Why not? What have I got to lose? If not this year, then when?*

I thought it would be simple, easy, and fun. I had not expected that such a simple project would confront me with important questions about how I wanted to live the second half of my life.

I purchased a book on how to make a gingerbread house and got started. Baking the pieces of the house went well. I moved on to the recipe for royal icing, carefully measuring the ingredients: powdered sugar, meringue powder, water. I whipped these ingredients at the required speed for the required amount of time. Because I had been so precise, I was sure that when I held up the whip, the icing would stand in the straight, stiff peaks essential to glue the house together and ensure it would not collapse. Instead, the icing slowly curled over.

I threw out that first batch of icing and repeated the measuring and whipping prescribed in the book. No stiff peaks. I tried recipes I found on the internet. No stiff peaks. Eventually, I settled for what I decided were stiff enough peaks. After a lot of trial and error and frustration, I finished assembling the house on a plywood board. It did not collapse. However, it was crooked and spattered with royal icing—a bit like my kitchen counter, the kitchen floor, my clothes, and my hair.

Frustrated and discouraged, I considered giving up. In my desire to rekindle the elation I experienced as a child when I mastered something challenging, I failed to take into account the many trial and error experiments required to grasp a crayon and draw those skies with puffy white clouds, a yellow sun, and a rainbow. I preferred to remember the joy of being a child, calling everything I had done as a child "PLAY" — fun and easy.

I had not bargained for feeling inadequate, frustrated, and discouraged. After many years of learning and practice in a variety of areas, I typically found myself on the middle or higher rungs of most skill ladders. I had forgotten what it was like to be at the bottom of the skill ladder: a beginner.

I realized there would be no problem with abandoning the project. There was nothing at stake: not money, not grades, not certification, nothing that would harm me or anyone else. That understanding had given me the freedom to begin the gingerbread house in the first place. I was free to give up on the project and avoid the uncomfortable feeling of being a beginner again. Was that how I wanted to live the second half of my life?

It would take time to answer that question. What I knew with certainty is that the spell of enchantment cast by remembering my delight in mastering something new would not let me give up. I continued working on the project, deciding I probably wouldn't take it to the show.

Without the pressure of feeling I had to create something prize-worthy, I began to enjoy experimenting with different ways to accomplish the tasks detailed in the book. Some worked, some didn't, but I finally finished the house. After swirling royal icing across the board to create a snowy landscape, I stood back to see the result of my efforts. The house was only a little bit crooked. Yes, it was spattered with royal icing, but I could take a wet paper towel and wipe some of it away. Studying the house in more detail, I found myself delighted with the red, green, yellow, and purple gumdrops that served as Christmas lights. Small bits of red licorice shaped into bricks made a very charming chimney, chocolate nonpareils, a nice snow-covered roof, and a mixture of melted marshmallows, cornflakes and green food coloring formed beautiful evergreen trees. The house was far from perfect, and it would not win any prizes, but it was good enough.

I took it to the Gingerbread House Show. The staff and the other creators at the show were as supportive as any preschool teacher, praising my efforts and asking me how I created the evergreen trees.

Long ago, I had decided that I had no choice but to be a spectator. I thought that only people who had natural ability for art had the right to display their talents. It was a revelation to create something that was only "good enough" for the pure fun of it and receive praise for my efforts by those who were far more experienced.

I had not only rekindled my delight in mastering something new, I had also rekindled the humility necessary to become a beginner again, humility that required me to accept being at the bottom of the skill ladder, humility that required me to accept myself as a work in progress instead of judging myself against those with more experience. Humility to accept that frustration, and other uncomfortable feelings, were an inevitable part of a beginner's experience. Those uncomfortable feelings made the moment of standing back to see the results of my efforts particularly rewarding. If I could embrace the beginner's humility, I knew that I would be able to become a beginner again and again in the second half of my life. After all, why not? What have I got to lose? If not now, when?

***

Terry Northcutt is a Guided Autobiography Instructor who works one-to-one with people of all ages to help them write their life stories. At seventy years of age, she is currently embracing Beginner's Humility to become a certified book coach to help writers complete memoirs, novels, and nonfiction self-help books.

2

What Matters Most

by Con Hurley

I am thirty-eight years old, sitting on a lonely Ireland hillside. Before me is Dunmanus Bay stretching out into the broad Atlantic. The hill I sit on is part of the rocky spine of a peninsula that separates Dunmanus Bay from Bantry Bay in southwest Ireland.

I am here to say goodbye. Goodbye to a ten-year dream that has ended in financial disaster and, towards the end, a faltered suicide attempt. The low ebb in the tide of my life as I gaze around the 230 acres that were to be my dream farm and home. A sad, sad moment.

As I pick up a fistful of loose soil and let it percolate through the sieve of my fingers, the sadness, guilt, and failure seem to follow the particles of soil and are replaced with something else. It doesn't take long for this something else to crystallise in my mind. Feelings of lightness and peace come over me.

Then the magic occurs. Slowly the sadness retreats. My taut mental muscles relax. I grab another fistful of earth and watch the particles trickle down slowly to my feet.

More thoughts emerge. The soil. The earth. I had always been fascinated by the magic of planting lettuce or cabbage seeds and watching the miraculous rows of tiny green leaves emerge. I began to look forwards; I was living in a house with a large back garden where I could grow plenty of vegetables.

A new dream was forming, one in which my wife, Eleanor, and our three children were centre stage, and I could still pursue my love of the land, only this time with vegetables instead of cattle and sheep.

And that's what I did.

My gaze shifted to the countryside around me, and I realised that I didn't need to own a farm and a flock of sheep to indulge my love of walking hills and mountains. All I needed was a good pair of hiking boots, a knapsack, and a raincoat, and I could walk the wilds of Ireland and abroad. So I bought the boots, the knapsack, and the raincoat.

As I left the West Cork farm behind me on that sunny day, I knew that this final visit represented a major turning point in my life. For the first time, I was absolutely clear about what was most important for me: the relationships I had with my wife and children and close relatives and my own health and happiness.

That was all of thirty-five years ago, and I can now reflect in a meaningful way on the effect and consequences of that fork on the hillside track.

The immediate effects happened virtually automatically. I turned my back, metaphorically and physically, on the failed farming venture and immersed myself in what was most important to me. I spent more time with my wife and family. I bought a used trailer tent and we toured Ireland and Europe together. I erected a plastic tunnel in the garden and grew a selection of vegetables inside and outside. Fresh vegetables with no air miles became the norm in our home.

For the first time, I was really part of our family. Of course, I was still travelling a lot in my work as an agricultural feature writer. But when I was at home, I was at home, except when I was walking with family and friends. I "owned" the hills and mountains of Ireland, Austria, the UK, and France for the price of a pair of boots.

Initially, I had focused on becoming a highly competent feature writer about dairy farming. But then I realised that milk production was not just about cows, grass, and profits; no, it was primarily about people---the families who milked the cows and reared the children.

The concept of "what matters most" crept into my work, and I switched to writing about farm families and then became a life coach. It has always been a thrill helping people work out what matters most for them and then put plans in place with strategies to achieve their goals.

In recent years, as I looked back to that pivotal moment on the hillside, the concept of what matters most began to stand out as perhaps the most crucial concept in helping people, as well as myself, to make more effective decisions. Of course, back then, I knew that marriage and family were important. But that was a different sort of knowing than being absolutely clear that they were what mattered most to me.

Over time it has become clear to me that I have created this life by the decisions I made in the past, and that my future life and happiness are being created by the decisions I make every day. Before putting the what matters most concept into practice, I had not made decisions that really reflected the importance of my marriage and children as well as my mental, physical and financial health. No. I had made decisions and allocated my time and resources to things that were of lesser importance.

Perhaps I was fortunate that the farm went belly-up and my eyes were opened. That turning point led to a mental shift from confusion and lack of clarity to a situation where I became crystal clear on what matters most to me in life.

Writing this essay has brought home to me the critical need for people to identify what matters most to them. I believe that this inward thinking work should be done early in life and repeated very often. Don't wait like I did, confronted with a financial crisis. I was fortunate that it was just money that I lost. I could have lost what mattered most to me. But I didn't, and I am forever grateful for that lightbulb moment on the hill overlooking the Atlantic Ocean in West Cork.

***

Con Hurley lives a happy, contented, and flourishing life in Cork, Ireland, with his wife, Eleanor. They have three children and eleven grandchildren. In his professional life, Con worked as Dairy Editor for

The Irish Farmers Journal *before becoming a Life Coach, public speaker, and course presenter. Con still grows vegetables and spends a good deal of time in the company of the people and hills that are dear to him.*

3

Heart Led

by Carol Henderson

W hen I first got pregnant in 1982, my husband, Bill, and I were
living in a cramped third floor walk-up apartment in Greenwich
Village. We barely had room to spread our arms. Our raised loft bed,
accessed by a steep ladder, allowed for a small desk underneath. How
could we add another person to our tiny space?

Though we'd been married for six years, we weren't big on making
plans. A few years earlier, we had moved to the West Coast with only
two duffel bags, our backpacks, and a few contacts. Did we want to raise
a baby in the city?

Relocating to a town on the train line between NYC and Boston – that
was the answer. My husband worked in both cities as a freelance writer. I
trusted I'd be able to somehow keep my marketing job in NYC. We chose
a sleepy coastal town in Rhode Island, a place we had visited and liked.
Most importantly, the train station was close by.

We took the Amtrak up in April and bought a small house in a day.
Not a great house, not even a good house – few closets, stuffy rooms –
but adequate. And with lower monthly payments than moving to a large-
enough city apartment. We had wanted to rent, but my mother, a tycoon
real estate broker, was adamant that we buy our first house. I was due in
September.

That summer, we devoted ourselves to renovating, tearing down walls
(well, others did that), scraping wallpaper, sanding floors while my

tummy grew bigger and bigger. The due date loomed large over the construction project. As a child, I hated the endless home improvement projects that my family constantly undertook. For a while, I even conveniently developed hives when exposed to paint fumes. But we were starting a family. There was work to be done, a nest to prepare.

Finally, the house was ready enough – the nursery walls painted a soft tangerine, appropriate for either sex, and after a forty-hour labor that progressed toward Cesarean, voila, Malcolm entered the world, scoring a ten on the APGAR test. "Perfect," the doctors said.

Three days later, Malcolm and I were preparing to check out of the small county hospital when our pediatrician appeared – he'd been away on a fishing trip. He took one look at our son and said, "This baby needs to be seen by a specialist immediately. His color is off."

Then he vanished.

I called Bill, who was painting the kitchen trim. "Come, right now," I said, my throat tight as taffy.

Malcolm did look a little gray, but what did I know? He often spit up after breastfeedings and made grunting sounds when he breathed, which I found endearing. Within the hour, he was yanked from my arms and rushed by ambulance to a larger hospital in Providence.

My husband and I followed as soon as the nurse removed my incision stitches, earlier than planned.

"Who knows when you'll be back," she mumbled.

As we entered the morose Victorian hospital, I could not believe that my baby, fresh from my warm, watery womb, was already inside this monstrous place without me. We found him, naked under glaring lights, tubes in many orifices, a square of his strawberry blond hair shaved for an IV, his arms and legs cuffed in gauze, secured to a padded table. Flanked by screaming babies, Malcolm lay spread-eagled, silent.

He seemed so wise, everyone said. We learned later that he probably didn't have the energy to scream. After myriad tests and much speculation, the doctors discovered a severe rare heart defect, only found in one in a million babies.

Hospitals, illness, and death terrified me. The worst ailment I had ever suffered was a full-body case of poison ivy. I avoided visiting sick friends or showing up for those who were grieving. I didn't write condolence notes. Now, a whirl of beeping machines, fluorescence, doctors, nurses, and babies dying beside our very sick one became the horror of my every minute.

But I couldn't turn away.

So many emergencies. A meningitis outbreak sent us home with Malcolm, the risk of exposure in the hospital too great. For two weeks, we stayed in our sparkling house, endless charts that tracked meds, weight, pees, poos, and spit-ups littering the crisp counters. The old-school visiting nurse folded her arms over her chest, declaring, "Such a sick baby should never be at home." She scowled on hearing about the vomiting, rashes, weird chest noises, my sleeplessness, and our frantic trips to the emergency room. Eventually, yet another ambulance took our son, me strapped in beside him, to an even larger medical center.

Malcolm had his first open-heart surgery at Boston Children's Hospital when he was five weeks old. Dr. Aldo Castaneda, our world-renowned surgeon, told us he had tried a pioneering surgery never used before. And it worked.

Medical professionals of all kinds paraded through our area in the Intensive Care Unit, congratulating us. Utterly spent from my 24/7 vigil, grabbing sleep here and there on couches in smoky parent lounges where TVs blared, I began to feel a slant of hope.

We were heading out of the ICU back to our new home with our "miracle" baby, who was pink and plump and would "one day grace the cover of *Time Magazine*," a doctor told us, when the heart valve repair failed.

Our boy turned the color of skim milk, and for the first time, raged against the needles and fluids and prodding he had tolerated before the first surgery.

Somehow I believe he knew.

He died the next day during his second open-heart surgery.

"There are support groups for parents," said Lydia's mom, another cardiac-kid parent who had paced the same sterile corridors.

"Not for me," I told her. Never. I was a private person, brought up to carry my grief and the shame of my gargantuan emotions alone. I had seen enough of my own and other people's suffering.

My husband and I returned to a house strewn with sweaty onesies, charts, and now useless medicines standing sentinel in the fridge. Overnight we realized we had no reason to stay. We decided to sell the place, whose bright, cheery walls seemed to mock us. The day we left for good, the furnace conked out. Fitting, I thought. The frigid January gloom quickly filled the rooms.

What I didn't know then, of course, was that after three moves, two healthy daughters, and settling into my husband's cramped childhood home, I would sit at the kitchen table in the pre-dawn quiet to write a few more parenting essays for a light-hearted collection I was working on. Instead, the story of Malcolm poured out of me and became the memoir, *Losing Malcolm: A Mother's Journey Through Grief.*

At the end of each book reading, I would look into the ravaged eyes of bereaved parents who approached me, searching for answers.

"Write," I would say. "Write and share your story."

That's all I knew to tell them.

I began to teach writing, often in medical settings, often with the chronically ill, the grieving, the broken – those whose unbearable stories clamored to be written and shared.

***

Carol Henderson is a writer, teacher, and workshop leader who has taught in the United States, Europe, and the Middle East. She has published two memoirs, written widely for magazines and newspapers, and has edited several memoirs and essay collections. She specializes in using writing as a tool for healing.

4

Luck: Do We Know It When We See It?

by Katrina Anderson

Y ou know that expression, "Timing is everything"? I believe that. In fact, it seems to be the unspoken credo of my life. Not because of planning, lord no. It's been luck, mostly just dumb luck.

My mother always told me, "It isn't a matter of luck—anyone can have that. It's a matter of what you *do* with that luck that matters."

Wise words from a wise woman. But another aspect to luck is timing. The ability to actually *know* when it's luck and timing. Sometimes when things are chaotic, irritating, repugnant, or even boring, it is hard to—you know—see the forest for the trees. To actually see the luck and timing through the surrounding emotions.

In 1990, I was laid off from my job as an electro-mechanical draftsperson—on *drawing boards,* mind you! Computers were just starting to peer out from under the modern, massive industrial world. So I decided to take a certification course in a now-defunct, multi-platform network operating system called Novell Netware. The nascent networking industry seemed a good bet to try for my aspiring career, and at the time, the State would pay for the training.

I diligently went through three months of training and testing and then finished up with a certification in something for which I had zero hands-on experience. I certainly hadn't thought about that before, and the thought of going out to "sell myself" as a network engineer left me cold.

However, I knew of a then-fledgling veterinary school and hospital, an hour west of where I lived at the time, and found out that they were using a two-server, brand new, and utterly unreliable Novell networking system, linked throughout the entire campus and hospital. I also knew they had only one network person. Maybe he would let me follow him around.

He agreed. And for the first three days, we sat in his office while the phone constantly rang. He carefully put each call on hold without ever picking up. My hair stood on end as I realized he was ignoring every call for help at that institution.

After three days of this, though, the worst blow came. He quit. Just walked out and left the school. He left me all alone in a busy college and hospital with two major servers going down at least every three to four hours, twenty-four hours a day.

The people in charge begged me to stay and fill in, "at least for a few days."

Me, with no hands-on experience, only a piece of paper stating that I was "certified." My instincts wanted to run for the hills, but in good conscience, I knew I had to try to help.

This turned out to be a tectonic moment for me, though I certainly didn't know it at the time.

They gave me an office, my first real office … right next to the pig paddock in the large animal part of the hospital. The smell alone should have given me an idea of what was coming.

I shared the office with a German resident at the hospital who made sure to tell me dreadful stories of working there, as well as how everyone hated the new network and all the others who actually supported the dreaded machines. Cursed be the "network administrators," for they bring unwelcome, unreliable methods of critical communications.

When I would rush out of my office to put out yet another fire, I invariably had to pass the goat paddock. Goats are smart and quickly came to know me as that Scurrying, Stressed-Out Human Animal. They would rush in the direction that I was scurrying and bleat at me with raucous barks, their piercing golden eyes staring archly at me.

Eventually, I befriended the goats, who always gathered around me in great sympathy to hear my traumas, their tails flicking in support. They would never think to mention how everyone there hated the new network and its administrator. The goats were the biggest champions I had.

This job was singularly the worst experience I have ever had. Period. For three months, I was on-call 24/7, my home an hour away. I never actually knew what I was doing—but when it came to the networks and using them, no one else did either. Tears and wide-eyed panic were a daily necessity. I would get home at six in the morning, my beeper would go off at 6:30, and I would be in my car again by seven, heading back for yet another urgent server crash.

I was so sleep-deprived early one rainy morning that I hit (or gently bumped) a man crossing in front of me at an intersection in my neighborhood. Thank heaven he was okay. But it wasn't just the servers crashing. My world was crashing too.

But I learned … oh, how I learned. I learned that I was resourceful, resilient, and really could think under pressure. I could keep going when all I wanted to do was quit or die. And most importantly, I kept my love of animals and sense of humanity close to my heart, no matter what monstrous development fell into my lap, intent on my demise.

At the end of this agonizing experience, I knew I could either let everyone know how dreadful it had been, how miserable I had been there, and how their management was nothing more than chaos, or I could be kind and good-humored about it, praising my colleagues for their patience and willingness to work with me. It had been a profound experience that provided me with a true gift: the gift of learning what I am truly made of. I damn well needed to rewrite my inner report of that experience, this time with grace and gratitude.

Afterward, I snagged a great network engineering job at a large hospital in Boston, never using Netware again in my entire career. With regular hours, good pay, and lots of support, I was able to take the local MBTA subway from my home to the hospital every day.

So—was I lucky? Was the timing of this experience unbelievably good fortune? Absolutely. Did I know it at the time? Absolutely not.

But you can bet that I do now.

***

Katrina Anderson is a Midwesterner who has lived in Massachusetts for forty-seven years. She's been writing and reading stories all her life, but only since taking Guided Autobiography classes did she start to sheepishly share her pieces for others to read. She lives on Cape Cod with her husband and two mongrels, Maudie and Pip. She loves all of them most dearly.

Number 47

by Bill Marsella

L ike a lot of eighteen-year-old college freshmen that evening in
1969, I was anxiously watching the television as CBS newscaster
Walter Cronkite slowly pulled small plastic cubes out of a large tumbler
and read the numbers printed on them. This was no national game of
Bingo, it was the first time the nation held a lottery for the military draft,
and my birth date was one of 365 cubes in the mix.

The Vietnam war was in full swing and, like many of my generation, I
was not excited by the prospect of being drafted into the military. I was
so anxious I had to leave the TV set while my younger brother Bob
watched instead. Then I heard him shout, "Billy, I see your
birthday...you're number...forty-seven!" My heart immediately sank, and
I knew that upon completion of my studies I would be drafted into the
United States Army.

Three years later, on June 8th, 1972, I received my diploma from the
University of Minnesota with a B.A. in Social Work and Psychology—
and one week after that, I received a letter from Uncle Sam ordering me
to report for active duty to Fort Leonard Wood, Missouri on August 22nd
to begin my basic training.

My wife Cathy was pregnant with our firstborn, and as I boarded the
plane, I was filled with anxiety knowing that we would be apart for at
least the next eight weeks. Once the plane landed, those of us who were
new Army recruits boarded a train for the ride to the base. We were

herded together like cattle, and I remember thinking, I wonder if this is
what it feels like to go to the slaughterhouse.

I was assigned to Company B of the 3rd training battalion. I had
resolved to mind my own business, to just blend in with the crowd and
get through the next eight weeks so I could move on to my advanced
training at Fort Sam in Houston, Texas as a social work/psychology
specialist in the Army Medical Service Corps.

Two days into boot camp, our platoon of thirty men were put on KP
duty—or 'kitchen police' for you civilians. We were busy washing pots
and pans when one of my fellow soldiers lifted a hot tray from the stove
and turned, not knowing I was standing behind him. He caught me under
my face and my chin was burned. I was taken to the ER on base, where
the physician applied salve and then wrapped my chin from ear to ear
with white gauze padding. The next day, our Drill Sergeant called us into
formation. There we stood, thirty young men all in the same solid drab
uniforms, a sea of olive green save for one large white speck in the
middle of the group.

It was exactly what I did not want—to stand out. Sure enough, Sgt.
Butts started referring to me as "Chin," and one day after marching drills,
he pulled me aside.

"Chin, I understand you completed college. Is that true?"

"Yes, Drill Sergeant."

"What did you study?"

"Social Work and Psychology, Drill Sergeant."

"Good," he said, "How would you like to be my Platoon Leader? Half
of these mother (expletive deleted) dropped out of high school and got
their girlfriends pregnant, and the other half are drug addicts."

"What does being a Platoon Leader mean?"

He said, "You get your own private room and no extra duties."

"I'll take it!"

For the next eight weeks, I led my platoon calling "cadences" on long
road marches, helped get them to the right place and at the right time for

training exercises, and sat up at night talking with those who were having problems adjusting to life in the Army.

Being thrust into the role of Platoon Leader that fall was my first real leadership experience and started me on a wonderful 33-year military career that led me to attain the rank of Lieutenant Colonel. I trained a company of soldiers who went on to successfully complete two tours in Iraq, providing much-needed mental health services to soldiers on the battlefield.

When I think back on the profound positive impact military service had on my life and the life of my family, I realize how fortunate I was to have been born on November 11th and to have that lottery number picked that fateful evening in 1969. My service in the military, like so many other veterans will testify, was a significant "branch" in my tree of life. I've come to realize that sometimes, in order to realize the full benefit of a life's branch, you have to "go out on a limb," whether by your own intention or—as in my case—by the luck of the draw in a draft lottery and an unexpected accident in an Army mess hall.

***

Through his long career in the Army Reserve Medical Corps and as a professional fundraiser for charitable causes, Bill Marsella discovered his passion for helping people share their life stories so that they know their lives have made a difference and will be remembered by future generations. A trained Legacy Facilitator and certified Guided Autobiography Instructor, Bill now dedicates his time and talent to helping others share their life's legacy.

The Big Interrupter

by Pam Toal

I t started with a flutter, like a tiny butterfly slowly flapping its wings for a few seconds and then going still. It reminded me of being newly pregnant when I'd wonder, *Was that the baby moving?* I knew that particular scenario was impossible because a) I hadn't had sex in forever and a day, and b) I was turning fifty soon. But I knew the occasional flutter in my abdomen was unusual and made a mental note to talk to my nurse friend, Holly, about it when I visited her in a few weeks.

Toward the end of that languidly long weekend spent talking and laughing and watching our teenage girls do the same, it was time to seek Holly's advice. As we strolled through her bougainvillea-filled San Francisco neighborhood, she said, "Pammy, I think you should have it checked out. It's probably nothing, but you'll feel better knowing if anything's going on."

Back at work the next Monday, I gently closed my office door and flipped open my phone. I had a busy week ahead of me---speeches to make, a board meeting to attend, funding applications to review. A typical week for me. I was a United Way executive. It was a big job that I seemed to enjoy growing even bigger by launching initiatives and forming coalitions to address issues like homelessness. I loved being a leader and making a difference. I definitely didn't have time to be sick.

My hands shook as I pressed the numbers on my phone to call my family doctor. I was able to see her the following week in a windowless exam room, its yellow walls adorned with jungle animals. After listening to me describe my butterfly symptom, she said she didn't want to speculate and ordered blood tests. Within a few days, I got a call at work from her nurse. "Can you come in to talk with Dr. Powell soon, perhaps tomorrow?"

The next morning, I learned the test results pointed to cancer, and I was referred to an oncologist. I had heard people describe cancer as the Big C, a journey, the club you're instantly a member of but you never ask to join.

My mom died of brain cancer when she was just thirty-nine. I was a single mom of two teenagers with a big job and a long life that I wanted to live. I was terrified, and I had a lot of meetings on my calendar. How could I sit in a chair and act normal?

Within a week, I found myself in another windowless exam room, this time with a pale male oncologist with a comb-over that smelled of aftershave. In a low monotonous voice, he told me I had stage three follicular non-Hodgkin lymphoma, that it was treatable but not curable, and that some of his patients had lived five years.

He handed me a brochure and suggested I join a clinical trial. In my head, I was screaming, *I can't even spell this disease, how can I decide anything?* Resisting the urge to flee, I stumbled out of there as soon as he quit talking, eventually finding my way to the clinic's parking garage. I have no idea how I got home.

My diagnosis tilted the axis of my universe at home, at work, in my relationships, everywhere. It was my work life that yielded the biggest surprises. Even though I could still be myself with my family and friends, I did not know how to be myself as a female community leader with cancer. For starters, with six rounds of chemo, it was inevitable that my hair would fall out, clump by clump. As if women don't already have enough hair issues!

Fortunately, my son came home from college one rainy weekend. Knowing his steadfast nature, I asked, "Will you please shave my head after dinner?" I'd purchased a mousy brown wig in an attempt to replicate my current professional woman look. I hoped I could pull it off.

The kindness bestowed on me from my staff, board members, business leaders, elected officials – everyone I interacted with in my work life – was profound. I knew people would be nice. I just didn't know a CEO in my Rotary Club would beg to do my ironing, or that the food bank director would sit with me during my three-hour, blood-red, poison-dripping chemo infusions, or that another nonprofit exec would insist on gifting me the hundreds of dollars my daughter needed for a good stove to launch her catering business.

Over time, I learned to accept their love. And even so, after joining that clinical trial to survive cancer, after staying in my position another two years where I'd once again happily ramped up my busy meter, I decided to leave my job. I needed to leave even though I was appreciated and admired, and compensated well, and all that. I needed to leave a job most United Way executives never leave.

But I had given what I had to give, now I wanted a quieter life. My kids were grown and doing well. The man who'd proposed to me turned out to be afraid of my cancer and flew off to the Arizona desert to golf.

I was free to do whatever I wanted.

I sold my house and moved a hundred miles south to Portland. I walked the city's leafy neighborhoods, ate at farm-to-table restaurants, and met young people with full arms of rainbow-colored body art. I enrolled in a coach training school, got certified, and started a business. Soon I began to miss my peeps, and moved back home after a year.

I received Gates Foundation funding to coach nonprofit leaders. If not for the Big C, the big interrupter of my career, I would not have found a new calling. I'm now sixteen years out from my original diagnosis, and I try to be open to life's interruptions.

***

Pam Toal is a writer, coach, entrepreneur, and certified Guided Autobiography facilitator. Her background in nonprofits, higher education, and consulting led her to discover the rewards of sharing life stories. In her spare time, she enjoys gardening, hiking, and dreaming up adventures with family and friends.

7

My Covid Flu-cation

by Sarah White

I n the last week of October, I was exposed to Covid-19 through visits with my mother in a congregate living facility. She tested positive just before she passed from this life, but what took her down will go on record as respiratory failure of unspecified origin. I, on the other hand, will be counted in the great roll call of Covid statistics—happily, not among the dead.

My symptoms came on about two weeks after that known exposure. Because of the exposure, I had already gotten tested two times, five days apart—both came back negative. The first clue I was sick was a spell of unstoppable shaking after teaching a class over Zoom. I put it down to nerves about the new curriculum. The next day a headache and body aches followed. I put that down to a new yoga routine I was doing and a longer walk than usual. But by Friday, I had a fever of over 100, had lost my appetite, I hurt all over, and food tasted different.

I went to the clinic for another Covid test, cleared my calendar, and prepared for the unknown.

Saturday, the third test came back negative, but a new symptom appeared—a steady stream of post-nasal drip. Soon my dry cough turned into a wet, sleep-disrupting mess. On Monday, my doctor prescribed antibiotics after a telehealth visit. By Thursday, I was at the clinic in person, suspecting pneumonia, which a chest X-ray confirmed. Friday— twenty-five days after my last known exposure—I finally tested positive.

And so began my Covid "Flu-cation." I've been self-employed for most of the last 20-plus years; I don't take a lot of time off. To permit myself two weeks off in a row, I generally have to leave the country. Doing nothing for weeks on end in my own home was a brand new lifestyle. To be released from striving felt rare and wonderful.

Sleep was my only interest—my hobby, my passion. I couldn't stand to wear anything but stretchy pajamas, knowing that at any moment, an irresistible urge to return to bed might overtake me. At odd times I would wake hungry, but no food sounded good, and I found it difficult to finish even an egg or a slice of toast.

Oddly, while I couldn't summon the brainpower to even think of doing any work, I found I could read and listen for pleasure. I pulled random children's books off the shelf and re-read old favorites. I listened to podcasts. I simply slept, entertained myself, and tried to eat and drink water, as advised.

I was tremblingly weak, and yet my Covid lifestyle was strangely enjoyable. My spirit floated somewhere above my suffering body, experiencing the days like shards of light piercing the dark. Hot baths became long moments of beauty as sunlight fractured on the surface of the bathwater and steam soothed my lungs. And afterward, to crawl back between the flannel sheets and descend into another sleep was purely a gift. There were other gifts—people brought groceries, sent chocolate, and emailed links to silly YouTube videos. My flu-cation was marked by generosity and compassion.

My daytime sleep was merely a loss of consciousness. Nights were a different world. I descended into fevers, sweats, long hours awake as my lungs crackled and wheezed. And when I did sleep, I entered a vivid place, peopled with streets full of performers in costumes, sometimes jugglers, sometimes marching bands, with an atmosphere like Carnevale. Night after night, I found myself returning to the same geography—an alternate version of the near east side of Madison. I had a definite sense that these crowds of people were other dreamers in their own COVID nights, and their dream messages were trying to reach us. We were all enrolled in some kind of wisdom school.

About two weeks into this fun-house dreamland, an episode came that felt like the culmination. I had become a motivational speaker aboard a cruise ship. The message I preached, received from Covid, was complex and beautiful and the rest of my life would be devoted to sharing it.

On waking, that complex beauty slipped through my brain cells like water through fingers. All I could capture of it were two phrases: *Be kind to each other* and *Elevate your daughters*. Not bad messages, but nothing compared to the spiritual beauty I felt lurking just beyond my ken.

In an essay titled "On Being Ill," Virginia Woolf wrote:

> Considering how common illness is, how tremendous the spiritual change that it brings, how astonishing, when the lights of health go down, the undiscovered countries that are then disclosed … it becomes strange indeed that illness has not taken its place with love and battle and jealousy among the prime themes of literature.

Because my Covid flu-cation came eighty years after the widespread use of antibiotics, it was over much quicker than illnesses in Virginia Woolf's time. Even so, it was an ellipsis, an omission from regular time. From the beginning of quarantine after my mother's positive test to the day the Public Health Department ascertained I was free to leave the house, thirty-four days had passed. When I went under, the world outside was still in the fall season, with sunny and improbably warm days. When I was reborn into the world, it was December and the world was dusted with frost crystals.

Thirty-four days is enough time for a physical, emotional, and mental reset. I have that disoriented feeling that comes when one returns from a long vacation: What is this place? And what is my role in it?

***

Sarah White is a freelance writer and personal historian. As a developmental editor, writing coach, and ghostwriter, she helps people write about their lives and work. She has taught more than 100 workshops in reminiscence writing, Guided Autobiography, and creative nonfiction. Sarah holds an MFA from the University of King's College.

8

Childless Thoughts

by Carolyn Young

C onsidering that Mom was the quintessential mother and grandmother, I grew up imagining the same for myself. I was the youngest in our sibship of three and was fascinated by children younger than me. As I look back from the perspective of age, I wonder how much of this was a desire to wield some authority over another, as my older brothers did when left in charge of me.

I loved to babysit, and in college I daydreamed with my steady about what we'd name our children. Although that romance faded, and I became invested in a pediatric audiology career, I could not imagine never having my own children. As I approached thirty, I took out a life insurance policy because I had established in my own mind that if I reached forty with no children, I would adopt; but that would be an age when insurance costs would be considerably greater.

One Memorial Day holiday, my older brother asked me to stay with his three young ones while he escaped with his lovely wife for a romantic four-day weekend. I loved the kids and was thrilled to comply. I'd never been in charge of young ones around the clock for days at a time, and after four days of constantly checking on a one, four, and five-year-old, I re-evaluated the parental prospects I wanted for myself. I'd never realized how parenting is 24/7, and I didn't much like being constantly on-call, even with kids as much fun as these were.

I enjoyed having my nieces and nephews visit one at a time, and they were fascinated at my apartment with the excitement of city life contrasting their suburban home. One of their biggest kicks was taking my trash to the top floor of my building and hearing the crash-bang of it bouncing off the walls of the rubbish chute all the way to the bottom. This was before recycling, and all the cans and bottles would create a mini-thunderstorm of racket.

I had another experience with day-long child care when my brother appealed to me to help his recently bereaved brother-in-law, whose wife had died in brain surgery, leaving five kids, ages one to twenty. My brother told me, "The father will pay you, and your helping out would give him time to find a housekeeper who will stay. Three have already proven unsuitable, and the kids are climbing the walls."

I was there from 7 am when the overwhelmed fifty-nine-year-old father left for work until he returned at 7 pm. He told me I was "a gift from heaven," and I had the three and five-year-old convinced that I was the American Mary Poppins, made more believable given my red umbrella that I claimed to be the means of drifting down to their home. The three young ones still at home were (and remain) dear to me. But full days of fixing meals, cleaning cupboards, running errands, mediating battles and such were definitely not something I looked forward to as I rose early to be at their home for their dad's departure and instructions.

In my early thirties, I was very aware of my biological clock winding down. A girlfriend whose courtship and wedding and first child were very much woven into my own life called from the maternity ward to tell me her second daughter had arrived by C-section. She spoke rapturously about how perfect the baby was and wanted me to be her Godmother. Then in the middle of her effusiveness, she said, "Oh, wait a minute. They just brought my pain medication." Her voice had not a note of pain, only immense thrill following the birth. When I questioned, "Pain?" she reminded me, "They just sliced me nearly to my backbone to get this one out, and you're my first call." How her rapture was ascendant over her pain left me in tears, wanting a baby so intensely I almost called an old flame in Indianapolis, whom I knew was always ready in the wings. I yearned to talk to my own mother but felt that such an admission would make her fear that I'd carry through with the single motherhood I'd talked about with her recently.

As I approached my imaginary adopt-at-age-forty "deadline," the prospect of adoption became less appealing. I was exposed to many children during the course of my work who were less than angelic. Parents would often compliment me on my patience when faced with an obstreperous child. "I don't know how you do it," they confided, "the kid makes me crazy!" I answered, "I don't go home with them."

I can call up short-term tolerance, but long-term is another story. Living with the kid would've made me crazy, too. I liked being able to retreat to the solitude of my apartment.

Another factor influencing me was that many age-peers approaching forty were having problems with their kids. I was always struck with two expressions: "When you have a child, you see your heart walking outside your body," and "You're never happier than your most unhappy child." Maintaining a healthy heart inside my body is more than enough for me.

All through my childbearing years, I never completely rejected the notion of having children. On the other hand, neither did I feel as if I'd met a partner who made a compelling and appealing marriage option, much less someone who would share the burden and joys of children so fully with me as to add to the quality of my life.

With childbearing behind me, the marriage imperative was lifted. I have always enjoyed time for myself as an adult. Now at the age of a grandparent, I've known many friends with children who have had to weather heartbreaking circumstances that vexed and hurt them as parents in ways that would be great fodder for *True Confessions*. While I sympathize with my close friends, I know I can only imagine and not fully feel what they must endure during their children's trials. I honestly don't know if I could have conjured up the resilience to weather such traumas. Of course, I somehow would have if circumstances had required it, but I very much doubt I'd have carried off the responsibilities without considerable resentment. I'll never know, and am thankful I won't have to find out for myself.

Over many years as a pediatric audiologist, I often thought to myself, "I've done more, for more, by having none." I've attracted enough *Sturm und Drang* in my own life; I do not, from this perspective, feel cheated having no children. Instead, I feel gratitude for the loves I've had and for the love I've given and the love that sustains me now with my husband, a few close friends, and dear family.

***

Carolyn V. Young, M.A., is a retired audiologist trained at Purdue and Northwestern Universities. She founded an Evanston-based private practice and coordinated audiology services for one of the out-patient clinics at The University of Illinois at Chicago. In retirement, Ms. Young volunteers for a virtual "village," WiseUp – Aging with Attitude.

9

Moving On

by Jo Ann Church

In September 1976, I was happily teaching at Malmstrom Air Force Base in Great Falls, Montana. For the past four years, five of us had worked for the VA teaching reading skills to young airmen to help them pass their on-the-job training, complete their GEDs or high school diplomas, or prepare for college English and math. Suddenly, that September, the VA decided to end the program.

September is not a good time to be an unemployed teacher.

After teaching part-time for a year and struggling to find full-time employment, I decided to try my hand at real estate. I enrolled in a week-long real estate course, took the exam, and was hired by a local firm to begin my new career.

It was a bitter cold January day when I showed up for my first day. The broker had assigned four of us to get some additional training before we started selling. The trainees included a retired Air Force colonel, a former cake decorator from a local grocery store, a very young former secretary, and me. Nothing quite prepared me for what followed.

We trainees had a booklet to read, from which the trainer asked us questions. I assumed, of course, that he was an experienced real estate agent who was going to quiz us on the booklet material and expand on the information therein.

Instead, here is how the sessions unfolded: Mr. Trainer would go to the chapter questions, select one, ask the group, and wait for an answer. No one would answer the question, and the others would just stare at him awkwardly. When I would inevitably break the excruciating silence by answering the question, Mr. Trainer would look up the answer at the back of the booklet, verify I was correct, and move on to the next question. These questions were basic and should not have been particularly difficult for anyone who had passed the real estate class or even read the booklet.

Anyone who has worked as a teacher knows ways to engage people in the learning process so that everyone can participate and reinforce basic facts. Unfortunately, Mr. Trainer did not make any attempt to involve the other trainees. In addition, he obviously knew nothing about real estate. Luckily, the training sessions were an hour a day and were over in a week. Done with training, I immediately became very busy learning how to sell homes by doing it.

Within a couple of weeks, my fellow trainees disappeared. I went on to outsell everyone in the office for the months of January and February. I attribute my success to a couple of factors. Beginner's luck obviously played a huge role. But I think being a teacher was my greatest asset. Teachers must learn early on in their careers to interact with all kinds of people. Many of our students reflect my fellow trainees and my clients in that they are unable or unwilling to talk and exchange information with people they don't know well. My second ace in the hole was my English teaching background: I still believe that if you can sell grammar, you can sell anything!

It would be nice if my story ended by my becoming a rich real estate baroness. But the reality was, I didn't like being in sales. I had three young children at home, and showing houses takes place in the evenings and on weekends, times I preferred to spend with my family. Another negative to real estate sales was that each week the broker ranked all the agents from highest production to lowest and posted the rankings outside his office for everyone to see. When I earned my place as a top producer, I became a threat to the other sales staff. In real estate, your co-workers are your rivals. I preferred the team spirit in education.

I found myself at a crossroads—use my teaching skills to succeed in real estate, or use my teaching skills to teach.

In mid-February, I applied for a position at a local college to develop a learning center similar to the one on the base. I was ecstatic when I got the position, and my real estate career ended in two months.

I later learned that Mr. Trainer was a former manager of an irrigation company and had no realty experience. I hear he was a friend of the broker.

***

Jo Anne Church is a retired English professor who still loves writing and teaching. Four years ago, she and her husband moved to beautiful Missoula, where they enjoy a multitude of cultural and outdoor activities with their friends and family.

10

A Wail on the Beach

by Jean Morciglio

I usually felt calm near the ocean, but not on that day. The sun was generous, and I could almost taste the salt in the air. Ocean birds wheeled overhead, squawking, colliding with each other as they dove to snatch things from the water. The ocean was busy, but I sat on a blanket, preoccupied.

After we'd unpacked our beach paraphernalia – towels, food, and tons of sunscreen – my husband and two sons took off. I had grown up on this beach in Puerto Rico but ended up raising my children in Michigan. This was their first visit to the ocean. My sons immediately noticed the crabs and grabbed buckets to capture them. I explained that crabs were not willing collectibles, but this made them even more interested, so off they went, their father following, in search of prey.

This was a well-hidden beach. Few tourists came here, but several families with small children had bunked down nearby. I tried to enjoy the ocean again, which had been so much a part of my growing up, but found myself still distracted by my problem at work.

On the shoreline in front of me, I watched a boy and a girl, probably his older sister, close to the same age as my kids, playing with a "boogie board." The small, lightweight fiberglass board was like a gateway drug to surfing, I remembered. This beach, Luquillo Beach, was perfect for that, with mild waves near the shore and stronger waves further out, for the more daring. The thin girl in a black-and-white striped bathing suit with a red sash, maybe a head taller than the boy, was showing him how to use the board. She rode the board along the shoreline, then dove dolphin-like in and out of the short waves while the boy ran alongside her on the beach.

I tried to enjoy this ocean scene, so reminiscent of my childhood, but my mind kept circling back to work. I felt like I'd done a good job. In my years at the college, I'd "progressed" from faculty to administration, increased enrollments, kept down costs, and even won awards for new programming. Weren't those the right benchmarks? Yet, that year, they'd hired a younger man in a position like mine. He was already part of a "breakfast club"– an informal daily gathering of deans and chairs, all men who'd been in the military. Recently, they'd posted a new leadership position, and the qualifications matched his background perfectly. No matter who applied for it, and they would encourage everyone to apply, especially minorities, he would be the "best fit."

Raised voices brought me back to the beach. A man, presumably their father, had joined them. He had the boy's arm in one hand and the blue nylon cord of the boogie board with the other. He gestured out towards the deeper water, where people were riding the wave breaks. They paddled their boards from a seated position, leaned forward, and rode the waves to shore – the next step in learning to surf. The man pulled the boy in their direction and insisted the girl let go of the board. When she didn't, he yanked it out of her hands, then headed to deeper water with the little boy dangling under his arm.

The girl followed her father and brother to deeper water, but the man turned and ordered her back to shore. *Why would he choose the poorer swimmer?* I wondered. The father's anger grew as the girl continued to follow him. He hollered at a woman on a blanket to my right, but she was occupied with a younger child. She made a half-hearted call to the girl, then turned her back and continued applying sunscreen to the toddler.

My mind went back to the problem at work. I could go to Human Resources. If I did, they might freeze the position while they explored whether they'd followed legal procedures. They might even re-write the posting. I might win that battle. But I knew if I did that, I would never see another good assignment or a promotion. If I stayed at the college, it would always be in dead-end jobs. I hadn't been in the military, but I knew that much about how things worked in the world.

Shouting on the beach caught my attention again. The girl yelled that she wanted to go along. The man turned on her, adding threats of curtailed privileges. When she still defied him, he raised his hand as though to strike her. This stopped her in her tracks. He headed out to the waves and left her standing alone in the water.

Instead of turning back, she leaned forward and let out a wail so loud that everyone on the beach turned to see what had happened. Her whole body shuddered, she clenched her fists and wailed again. She howled. Every part of her body was shaking. Her father looked back, then continued on, ignoring her. I looked toward the mother, but once she could see her daughter was not in any danger, she did the same. At first, I didn't understand. Was she spoiled? Was she over-reacting?

Then I remembered. Every girl has this moment but forgets it. The moment she realizes that the women in her life are not treated like the men. Her mother is not the same as her father, at home or in the larger world. She has the moment, then buries it. The women in her life will not tell her otherwise. As the girl continued wailing, I knew she was howling because of the unfairness of it. Because there was nothing she could do. A little brother would always be invited to do the things she really wanted to do, even if she was the better swimmer. Even though she had done everything she was supposed to. Even if she had earned it.

I got up and walked to the edge of the water. I had the urge to howl along with her, to scream – it's *not* fair! Or jump up and yell, *Take your daughter, she was here first.* Then finally, just to tell her the truth: it doesn't get any better when you get older. But I didn't say anything. I had learned to silence that voice a long time ago.

As the girl's wails subsided, I knew I would not go to Human Resources. I had always remained dutifully silent. But the energy behind that wail stayed with me. It also wasn't right to do nothing. I had to find something.

A few years later, when I became the Dean myself, I kept a picture of the ocean's wave-breaks on the wall in my office. People thought it represented tranquility.

***

A retired community college educator, Jean Morciglio teaches Life Story Writing and Adult Learning. She has a passion for providing students with the tools to define their own narrative and learn who they are in the process. She received the Florida Writers Association Gold and Bronze awards for memoir and fiction works.

11

He Gave Me My Life Back

by Gabriella Kelly-Davies

T he room swirled as my eyes fluttered open, and I could feel something tight around my neck. It felt like a vice, making it difficult to swallow. The antiseptic smell was familiar, but I couldn't quite place it. Struggling to focus my eyes, I heard a voice I knew well— it was Ben, a resident medical officer at Townsville General Hospital, where I worked as a physiotherapist.

"How do you feel?" Ben said, shining a bright torch into my eyes.

"Where am I?"

"You're in emergency. An ambulance brought you here because you were lying on the side of the road, unconscious. Your bike was a few metres away in the scrub."

Ben told me the ambulance drivers had received reports of people being pushed off their bikes at the quieter end of the beach. They assumed that was what happened to me.

That day, my twenty-fourth birthday, heralded the onset of daily migraines.

In the early 1990s, I was regularly travelling around Australia while studying business at night. About half an hour into each flight, pain like an electric shock would shoot up the back of my neck and head. It lasted for several minutes, followed by a deep ache in the base of my skull. The pain eventually spread upwards, fanning out until it covered the entire back of my head and temples. Within a few years, the pain I experienced on the plane became more regular.

In 1996, I started a job in Parliament House, Canberra. Each morning, I would feel shooting pains running up the back of my head, accompanied by waves of intense nausea. Soon afterwards, a deep ache in the base of my skull started, quickly spreading up over my head to my temples. My eyes felt gritty as if they were full of sand, and I yearned for them to explode to release the mounting pressure.

Often when the pain was at its worst, I couldn't think of the words I wanted to say. Embarrassed and losing confidence, I struggled to make my point, infuriating some of my colleagues. Sometimes I was unable to string two words together coherently. My mouth refused to form the words, as if the messages weren't getting through from my brain to the muscles in my face.

In 2005, my life changed. My doctor referred me to the world-famous Michael J. Cousins Pain Management and Research Centre at Royal North Shore Hospital in Sydney. On the day of my first appointment, I didn't want to get my hopes up too much because I'd been disappointed so many times, but I was still upbeat. Dr. Michael Cousins and a team of health professionals, including a physiotherapist, psychologist, social worker, and nurse, assessed me.

Dr. Cousins diagnosed occipital neuralgia, a form of headache. He said a whiplash injury was a known cause and occipital neuralgia sometimes activated migraines. In my case, it had transitioned to chronic pain.

Acute pain is the body's warning system that tissue damage has occurred, and it is a protective mechanism to prevent further injury. Acute pain is usually temporary and disappears once the tissues have healed. But sometimes, the pain goes rogue and transitions to chronic pain. Chronic pain is a malfunction in the way the central nervous system processes pain signals, rather than an indication of continuing tissue damage.

Dr. Cousins suggested an experimental new treatment he had successfully trialed on two other patients. It involved implanting tiny electrodes into the back of my head and neck to block the pain signals from travelling along the nerves in my head. I was willing to try anything, and despite feeling uncertain about the risks of surgery and the experimental nature of the treatment, I agreed to proceed because nothing else had worked.

And work it did, reducing the frequency and severity of my migraines. I felt as if Dr. Cousins had given me my life back!

One year later, while washing my hair, I felt something sharp sticking out from the base of my skull. It terrified me, and I immediately phoned the pain clinic. Fortunately, the nurse made me an appointment for the same day. When Dr. Cousins examined my neck, he said the end of an electrode had pierced the skin, and it was protruding through the back of my neck. Tests revealed that a staph infection had invaded the wires. He had no option other than to remove the electrodes and the pacemaker battery that powered them because it is almost impossible to clear an infection once it invades an implanted device. Afterwards, the migraines returned in full force, and the antibiotics made me nauseous. I despaired of ever living a healthy life again. However, three months later, Dr. Cousins implanted new electrodes. They didn't work as well as the old ones, but they did provide a baseline level of pain relief.

Disaster struck in 2008. A superbug infected the electrodes and wiring, forcing Dr. Cousins to remove them again. An infection control specialist started me on aggressive antibiotic therapy, and I felt as if my life was over. I wanted to die. Germs were my enemy. I obsessively washed my hands and cleaned all the surfaces in my room.

A significant turning point occurred in 2009 when I took part in ADAPT, a pain management program at the pain clinic. The program ran for three weeks, and each day psychologists gave lectures about chronic pain and tips on managing it. The physiotherapists started us on a carefully graded exercise program, and a psychologist taught us cognitive and behavioural therapy techniques to help us change the way we thought about and dealt with pain.

The program taught me to stop catastrophising and to believe I had the power to change how I reacted to pain. It was immensely beneficial, and for years I practiced the stretches and exercises every night after work. I also applied the psychological techniques for managing pain, such as desensitization, and they became central to my daily routine. I finally had more control over migraines and have never looked back—apart from a few rough patches when I trigger a flare-up by writing for too long, slouching, swimming too far, or carrying heavy shopping. One of the major improvements now is when I spark a flare-up, I use the skills I learned in the program, such as mindfulness meditation and carefully pacing activities and exercise.

My story illustrates several turning points that had profound implications for my future. I think of a turning point, good or bad, as a fork in the road. We have the opportunity to choose which arm of the fork we take.

***

Gabriella Kelly-Davies is a Sydney-based biographer enrolled in a Ph.D. program in biography writing. She recently wrote the biography of a trailblazing Australian pain medicine pioneer, Breaking Through the Pain Barrier: the extraordinary life of Dr. Michael J. Cousins. *Gabriella is President of Life Stories Australia, founder of Share Your Life Story, and runs life story writing groups.*

12

Monster and Angels

by Anita Wong Siew Ha

"Where, exactly, is Tanglin Halt Road?"

"It's in a new town called Queenstown. Our building is Block number 28, and the unit is 05-120. This means we are on the fifth floor, Unit 120."

"Wow, that's a lot to remember. I will write it down in my notebook."

Papa had finally decided we should move to a bigger place. I felt like the luckiest girl in the world!

Queenstown was located in a new precinct of our city nation. Each precinct was a new town of new public housing apartments, several stories high. It was clean, with modern facilities.

We were excited because now, instead of being tenants, we got to own our home. For eons, Papa had rented a small room – fifteen by twenty feet – in a three-story country house on Havelock Road. That was my birthplace. It took some creativity to squeeze all five of us in. I can't imagine it now, but amazingly we did.

Excitement mixed with trepidation when Papa decided to move me to a new school as well. That meant I had to leave my familiar village school, teachers, classmates, and favourite noodle stall. At that point, I wasn't sure if my excitement would last.

However, decisions were made, plans were drawn. We moved on March 10th, 1963. Fear and trepidation aside, the process of moving was still fun. I enjoyed tossing old stuff and getting new things. And best of all, I had a room just for my sister and me, a luxury after sharing a room for five.

What's more, we had our own bathroom and toilet. A new flushing toilet, not the ancient bucket system shared with five other families. I felt "modern" as I took the "lift" (elevator) downstairs and up again to go home. And neighbours were just a window away.

While I was happy waving bye-bye to the "old" and welcoming the "new," much of the new needed effort getting used to.

After weeks of paperwork, Papa had me transferred to Margaret Drive Primary School. Papa planned to bring me to and from the new school for the first three days. I was confident that I could manage after that.

The first day in my new school happened to be "Spelling Day." What luck! Mr. Tan, also known as "Monster Tan," was yelling out the vocabulary. We had to show our competence in twenty words. To pass his standard, no one was allowed to misspell even one word.

When the results were revealed, I was obviously the worst of the lot. The class had to pay dearly for my distorting the appearance of those words.

"All of you with words spelled incorrectly, step out and stand in a line! In front of me!" bellowed Monster Tan.

I was trembling as I stepped out with the rest of the offenders.

"What is he going to do? Will he make us run rounds? Stand on our chairs? Spank us?" A thousand questions were circling in my mind.

"Stretch out your hand and tell me how many times you deserve!" That thunderous voice disrupted my thoughts.

"Deserve? Deserve what?"

Soon, the answer was demonstrated. To my horror, I witnessed Monster Tan hitting my classmates' open palms with a ruler. The number of times corresponded to the number of words wrongly spelled.

That really freaked me out. I had only spelled three words right! By now, my eyes were blurry.

Fortunately, when it came to my turn, the "Monster" decided to be merciful. He signalled me to return to my seat. What a relief!

However, that incident never left me. I had always wanted to be a teacher. On that day, I resolved never to use fear to motivate students. Thinking back, I am glad that experience did not deter me from pursuing my dream. Monster Tan's fierce countenance is a constant reminder that love and encouragement is a better approach to inspire students to excellence.

After this episode, a mysterious experience followed on the fourth day. This was the day I had to bring myself home. I thought three days was enough to remember a new route. But I was wrong, so wrong! The way home turned out to be both a mysterious and unforgettable scare.

Going to school in the morning was a breeze. When the dismissal bell rang, I was ready to make my way home. Initially, my new friend Lay Khim walked with me. We were delighted to accompany each other. Soon, Lay Khim arrived at her home, and I walked on.

I was getting a little apprehensive walking alone. To keep a brave front, I hummed my favourite song. Suddenly, I noticed a change in the landscape. Houses started to fade. Instead, tall trees stood neatly on both sides of the road. The cement-paved road faded and a dirt path emerged. There was no sign of human existence around me.

"Oh, Mama! I'm lost!" By now, I was terrified.

I slumped onto the roadside. No one came. I really felt helpless. I sobbed uncontrollably.

Then, as if by divine providence, I saw three men walking towards me.

"Little girl, what happened?" One of them asked.

"I'm lost. I don't know how to go home!"

"Don't cry. We'll help you."

"Really?" I wiped my tears.

The three gentlemen conferred for a brief moment. The same one who spoke to me asked, "Do you know your address?"

"Yes, yes, uncle! My address is Block 28, Tanglin Halt Road, unit number 05-120." I read every word from my notebook.

"Good! Let's walk out to the main road and get a taxi."

I followed the three friendly musketeers expectantly.

Within ten minutes, we were at the door of my new apartment. Mama was shocked to see three men escorting me home!

"Mama! I was lost, and these kind uncles brought me back!"

"Oh my goodness! How could you get lost?! And thank you so much, kind gentlemen, for bringing my girl home! Please sit down and have a cup of tea."

"No, thank you, madam. We're in a hurry. Glad she's safe. Hey, little girl, be careful next time."

"Yes, uncles! I'll remember."

Yes, I remember their kind deed. Without them, I cannot imagine what would have become of me.

Since then, I have committed my address to memory and become more vigilant when traveling. Living in an urban housing estate is vastly different from living in a simple country house. I really missed distinctive landmarks like my favourite noodle stall that always pointed me the way home.

Still today, the sudden appearance of the three rescuers baffles me. How did they know I needed help, there and then? Could they have been my guardian angels?

***

Anita Wong, a recently retired missionary, presently resides in Singapore. She worked in Toronto, Canada from 2000-2020. She first attended a Guided Autobiography class in Singapore in 2013, and in 2017 earned her certificate to teach GAB herself. Since then, she has taught several classes in the Toronto area. Her hobbies include reading, writing, and traveling. She aspires to someday write a book.

13

A Life-Changing Moment (or "Movement")

by Ellis Waller-Walker

A fter I graduated from college, I was clueless as to what my career should be. I applied for every job and finally landed one as a waitress at a local restaurant. My poor parents weren't sure why I went to college or what type of skills I developed there. I wasn't sure why I went either, except that it was something to which everyone aspired. I remember taking my father to the airport and dejectedly asking him, "What am I going to do with my life now?" Without hesitation, he responded, "You will learn to live your life creatively!"

Creative living is not what came to mind when Emeline dropped the turd in my purse. I obtained a degree in Sociology and English and was committed to making a difference in society. It was the early 70's and we all felt compelled to "give back", "question authority," and to "make love, not war." We were the observers of Kent State, the protesters of the Vietnam War, and the supporters of McGovern. Working in a restaurant was okay, but it wasn't "giving back."

My mother helped me find a more meaningful job and suggested I volunteer in a nursing home. That's when Emeline dropped the turd in my purse, as I was waiting to speak to the Activity Director to see what type of assistance I might provide.

Emeline was a severely demented individual who couldn't speak and was scary looking, as she had severe contractures, was bent over, and couldn't communicate. Her wig was slanted on the right side of her head, and she was every young person's nightmare about growing older. One look at Emeline and most people would have thought they were in a horror film.

As I waited for Helene, a rather rotund, jolly, and loving person, Emeline turned to me with a hard dried-out turd which she held in her hands, unbeknown to the nurses' aides, and decided to gift it to me. Joy for joy. She dropped the turd in my handbag—the Greek shoulder bag that hung from my shoulder open at the top so that everything could be dropped in without too much fuss.

After talking with Helene and deciding that I was going to come in twice a week to conduct discussion and exercise groups with the elders, I went rushing home and couldn't wait to tell my mother what a gift I had received from Emeline. My initial reaction was, "I can't volunteer here!" But apparently, I was destined to work with seniors whether I wanted to or not.

After a few months of volunteering at what we used to call "convalescent hospitals," now euphemistically called "care centers," the California Board of Education in Huntington Beach started a new adult education program. They were paying teachers to go to these centers and teach exercise, social skills, and arts and crafts. Not only were they stimulating the minds of individuals who lived robust lives in the past, but they were stimulating their bottom line, as schools received funding from the state according to the number of students enrolled in a class.

It was easy to enroll a captive audience, and it was a creative challenge to develop educational activities which involved the minds of older adults who suffered from dementia, stroke, Parkinson's, and other diseases.

Because I didn't have a teaching credential, the Adult School encouraged me to enroll in some extra classes to receive a lifetime certificate which allowed me to teach at high schools and community colleges. I did so with great anticipation. Finally, I found the creative path that my father had encouraged me to explore.

The day I told the restaurant powers that I did not want to become a restaurant manager, I was offered a job with the Huntington Beach Adult School with the Program for Older Adults. Was this luck, fate, or the hand of God helping to guide my life? I wasn't sure, but I wasn't going to let this opportunity pass me by. Besides, it was also the year that the University of Southern California opened the School of Gerontology, to which I applied and got accepted. I just embarked on a road in my life that would forever change my future and direction.

So, you see, sometimes life gives you turds, but you shouldn't be discouraged because you never know what opportunities might come your way.

***

Following her "Life Changing Moment" and graduating from the first Gerontology class at the USC Leonard Davis School/Ethel Percy Gerontology Center, Ellis dedicated her life to teaching, developing gerontological curriculum, and establishing programs for seniors. Recently retired from Lifetime Learning Center in Seattle, Ellis founded Care Connections—a Social Adult Day Care Center, and held previous positions as an adjunct professor with Chapman University, instructor with Huntington Beach Adult School, and as Director of Education and Research with the California Association for Health Services at Home. She currently teaches online Gerontology classes at Coastline Community College.

14

Learning to Heal the Heart

by Jerry Waxler

I n 1970, I was living in a garage in Berkeley, California, supported by government programs for the poor, not speaking to anyone for weeks at a time. Floundering to make sense of my life, I attended a lecture at the university by the famous researcher Jane Goodall. After seeing her slideshow about the natural goodness of chimpanzees, I decided to emulate their basic lifestyle.

I switched to a fruit-only diet and stopped wearing my contact lenses. So, in addition to starving myself and being lonely, I was also legally blind. Though my physical heart was still beating, my reasons for living had collapsed.

I knew a lot about what keeps a heart beating.

Six years earlier, I had been a straight-A student in Philadelphia at one of the best public high schools in the country. Determined to be a doctor like my brother, I'd landed an after-school job at Temple Medical School's research center. When I wasn't washing bloody beakers and test tubes, I read medical textbooks. By the time I was ready for college, I could picture the precisely choreographed dance of nerves, valves, and chambers that kept blood pumping through the heart.

Because of my ambition and top college admission scores, I'd only applied to elite schools. On April 15th, 1965, a few weeks shy of my eighteenth birthday, every school had turned me down. In my mind, if you weren't smart, you were nothing. I had become nothing.

While quelling the scream arising from deep in my chest, I scrambled to find the best college that would accept me at this late date. Two months later, I flew from the East Coast to the Heartland—Madison, Wisconsin. A Jewish boy from a close-knit ethnic neighborhood, I had to make sense of this new identity in a state-sponsored college, with 30,000 students, most of them from the small towns and farms of Wisconsin, most of them of northern European descent.

Here hardly anyone cared about my great test scores, my proficiency in calculus, or my precocious absorption of medical textbooks. I was on my own, struggling to fit in. My focus on the physical heart had left me oblivious to the heartfelt connections between people.

I became increasingly lonely and increasingly desperate to understand why I always felt so bad. And since these were the years 1965 to 1969, all my thoughts were dominated by the strange, hypnotic maelstrom of the Vietnam war and the counterculture. I slid into the gravitational pull of the sixties like a planet falling into the sun. Soon I was stoned on marijuana most of the time, angry and frightened by war and power. I felt some fleeting sense of togetherness during the protests, but screaming together in mobs offered little warmth, leaving me just as lonely as ever.

Because adults had created this hated war, I came to see adulthood as the enemy. Embracing the nihilistic philosophies of the hippie movement, I turned my intellectual prowess toward self-destruction, rejecting everything I had been raised to believe, systematically teasing apart and dismantling the pieces of myself.

By the time I moved to Berkeley, California in 1969, I had nothing left. To make matters worse, I fell madly in love with a beautiful woman. When I discovered that I did not have the emotional skills to stay in a relationship, I was completely lost. Moving to the jungles of Central America and eating fruit from the trees seemed like my only remaining option.

That downward slide ended abruptly on an early spring day in 1971, when a friend handed me a photocopied chapter from a book about a spiritual path. I began my long climb back to sanity that day.

Unfortunately, it was not a simple process to pick up where I left off. I had already thrown so much away and had to start over.

In a long series of wonderful opportunities and hard work, I remade my life. Bolstered by supportive, nurturing friends and guided by wise, generous mentors, I meditated, wrote in journals, read self-help books, and dedicated myself to regular psychotherapy. I got married again. In 1997 at the age of fifty, I went back to school to get a master's degree in counseling psychology. Those courses opened my heart even more. By the time I graduated, I was eager to help people grow, just as I had done.

But when I tried to provide therapy, I realized I couldn't help people sort themselves out when all I could see in my early life was wreckage. I couldn't explain it, even to myself. That's when I discovered the miracle of memoir writing.

I began to recover the story of my formative years. Piece by piece, I picked up the fragments and placed them in order, attempting to describe the psychological ups and downs that led me from one place to another. The only mental process powerful enough to make sense of it all was the ancient system of Story.

I studied and wrote hundreds of essays about memoirs. By getting lost in each author's story and then stepping back to see how it fit in with all the others, I gained deep insight into the genre. Book by book, I learned the secret of what makes life worth living. During ordinary life, the wispy bits of joy, hope, and love float past and are quickly lost. But in stories, these tiny moments are the very thing that turn mere facts into moving, shared experiences.

Falling in love with memoirs and those who longed to write them, I began teaching classes and workshops, combining what I'd learned in therapy training with my discovery that memoirs are a royal road to understanding the human experience.

Through my association with groups of aspiring memoir writers, I learned yet another lesson. When someone shares a disturbing story, the group reaches out with supportive murmurs and softened eyes. Even modest first attempts to turn memories into stories shortens the distance between strangers. In those outpourings of group compassion, I was witnessing the birth of a kind of social connection I never imagined.

Looking back at my youthful devotion to medical textbooks, I see how I'd been so focused on the physical heart, I missed the potential for a different sort of life-sustaining health.

Now I see stories as the blood of civilization. Storytellers are its heart, pumping soulful joys and longings through the rest of our body. Every time I read a memoir, I feel bathed in the compassion of shared experience. In that sense, I guess I am a doctor after all. So is each person who contributes to the emotional health of our planet as they share their stories.

***

Jerry Waxler, M.S., speaks, coaches, and teaches about the individual and social healing described in his book Memoir Revolution. *His first memoir is about falling apart and coming together in the 60s. His currently unpublished memoir chronicles his midlife transformation from a math-loving nerd to a people-loving storyteller and listener.*

15

Loss & Change

by Robin Mintzer

My mother Helen's illness and death during my twenties was a major crossroad for me. Death and loss are common crossroads in general. But the devil is in the details.

I was almost twenty-three when she got sick, and she died two days after my twenty-sixth birthday. This experience for many years seemed so profound that I often likened it to the world's shift from BC to AD; life after her death was like living in a different millennium.

The loss of my mother hearkened a seismic change in my role in the family, my relationships within the extended family and friends, as well as my sense of self. Everyone saw me and related to me differently as I took on adult responsibilities – my mother's responsibilities. I believe people turned to me, in part, as a way of maintaining a connection with Helen.

Her passing unearthed a remarkable bevy of stories told to me by her friends: stories that exemplified what she meant to them and explained why so many emulated her. "Your mother was an inspiration and role model for me," they told me. I had only known my mom as she appeared through my eyes. Hearing about her through the eyes of so many others validated my experience of her as a person and as a woman.

I learned how to say goodbye – the forever kind of goodbye. She came home from the hospital because she wanted to die in our house. At some moment, my father told me that I needed to go and say goodbye to her. I don't know how to do this, I thought. I don't know what to say.

I dutifully went to her and told her that I loved her. It was a touching moment, but something was missing. Had I had more maturity and presence of mind, I would have told her things I appreciated about her. I wish I had done that. I resolved that, from that moment forward, I would tell everybody in my life what I appreciated about them. I would never wait until the final hour – that last moment. I have been doing this for forty years, and I think of my mother whenever I do so.

I learned how to ask for help. When she came home, I was the one who fed her. It seemed so wonderful – I had the privilege of cooking everything she loved and serving it to her. However, she didn't want any of it and rejected every sumptuous plate of her favorite foods. I kept trying to make it right. When she refused the crab salad – a bona fide perfect lunch – I reasoned that it wasn't fresh enough. I ran to the "better" fish store over the hill to get the very freshest crab, but the same response occurred. I was so exasperated, "Mom, you have to eat! You must eat for me." *Oh my, I just said that. How could I say that?*

When I left the room, I marched myself over to my dad and requested that he get a nurse or someone who knew how to feed her – this was well over my pay grade! Fortunately, he was able to do so, and the nurse, Mrs. Booker, made her scrambled eggs or mashed potatoes. She would feed her two to three teaspoons and mark down the number of ounces consumed. *So, that's how you do it.*

I learned how to negotiate gray areas and conflicts within my family. Part of my role included taking care of my maternal grandmother, who was 86 years old when the family moved into our "AD," our new millennium. It started out small – taking her to the market and to her doctors' appointments – and grew in stature and scale until I was making decisions about her life and her death. She was loved by many, and each person had an opinion about how things should be handled for her. I kept a keen eye on her and had my own ideas about what was best as her life moved forward.

Then there was the issue of peace in the family. I decided I would try to avoid going 'to the mat' as best I could. I made sure that everyone knew I would really listen to them before making a decision. That helped. But when there was a conflict, I spent goodly time explaining my opinion and rationale in an attempt to get others to see the situation through my eyes. Time and diligence paid off, and I never had a knock-down fight with anyone.

When I was getting married, many years after my mother's death, I visited her gravesite and told her, "Hey mom, I'm getting married." I sat and imagined her walking me down the aisle with my dad. In this vision, she walked with a pained and sickly gait. I was shocked to think that this was my image of her. I waited a bit and reentered the visualization. This time, she had an erect and confident gait. When we got to Dave, she and I hugged and kissed before she sat down, and she whispered in my ear, "He's a great guy!" I realized that I missed getting her blessing. With a shiver, I felt that, indeed, I did get it. She would have loved him. I still miss her deeply, and that is part of the grief process – it's always within us.

This life crossroad stands as a pivotal moment for me. I grew up fast. From this seismic shift, not only have I learned many foundational life lessons, but my sense of self in the world settled in. I do not fear grief or loss – not just as a survivor, but as a person – and one who honors them wholeheartedly. I can embrace uncertainty rather than tricking myself into finding solace in the past. I've become a more trusting person. I've become more forgiving – just a bit – as I still grapple with this. Her memory has helped me learn about forgiveness.

And I have forgiven her for leaving us so soon.

***

Robin Mintzer is a clinical psychologist in Southern California. In 2000, she became a Master Teacher of Guided Autobiography. Since then, she has spoken on GAB internationally. Robin has been with the International Center for Life Story Innovations and Practice (ICLIP) since 2001, serving on the Advisory Board for many years. She has been Co-Director of the Los Angeles Attachment Study group for over 30 years. Robin currently has a private practice in Newport Beach and is an Adjunct Professor at Pepperdine University.

16

Mother Tongue

by Lise Tétrault

I remember when I stopped speaking French, my mother tongue – the language of my heart.

It was October 1970, not long after I celebrated my sixteenth birthday. Up to that point, I had always felt at home speaking French. I would have liked to speak it with members outside my extended family, but I didn't hear it spoken in public places, and there certainly were no other teenagers in our rural community in Saskatchewan who spoke the language.

Being a minority Francophone had its limitations and its benefits. It afforded me an exemption from the mandatory high school French course and made me popular with my peers who needed help conjugating French verbs in homework assignments.

Passing the threshold of my sixteenth birthday was monumental! I was seriously exploring the larger world around me with the help of our parish priest, Father Bill Mahoney. Through weekly gatherings at Bill's house, my peers and I were introduced to the concepts of colonization and oppression. We explored the practice of liberation theology coming out of the Latin American countries which had been colonized by Great Britain, France, and Spain. These study sessions helped me to understand the role of colonization in the creation of poverty, oppression, and struggles for liberation. I was developing a growing understanding of how people with power and privilege used their money and influence to silence the poor by labeling them as terrorists if they dared challenge their authority.

As I grew to understand more about how the poor and oppressed of Latin America were living, I developed a greater interest in what was happening in the world. As I purposely listened to the news, much of what I was hearing was talk of the "terrorist Quebeckers." All media sources spoke of the "war" being waged in Quebec – a war portrayed as a fight between the French terrorists and the rest of Canada, who were all assumed to be English-speaking. The FLQ (Le Front de libération du Québec), a French-speaking political organization calling for Quebec's separation from Canada, was at the heart of the conflict.

The FLQ had been strategizing for years to obtain sovereignty for the Francophone people of Quebec. That year, their strategy included the kidnapping of a British Trade Commissioner to Canada and the Quebec Minister of Labour in an attempt to inspire the people of Quebec to reject the oppression of English dominance controlling the political and economic institutions within Quebec and to demand their independence.

Tragically, the FLQ's actions resulted in the accidental death of the Quebec Labour Minister. Fearing more unrest, Pierre Elliot Trudeau, then Prime Minister of Canada, enacted the War Measures Act, allowing the Canadian Government to deploy the federal army to Quebec. All individual rights and liberties within Canada were suspended as the Canadian army, together with the Quebec police force, were granted the power to raid homes and to detain and arrest without cause any individual suspected of sympathizing with the FLQ.

I remember feeling conflicted during those turbulent times. Like my relatives in Quebec, French was my first language. Over the years, as my parents' aunties, uncles, and cousins from Quebec had come to visit, we had created memories filled with laughter and joy. My maternal grandparents were often at the heart of the festivities. We would gather on their farm feasting and dancing as my grandfather played his favourite jigs on his harmonica. My extended family members from Quebec were such fun-loving, heart-filled people!

The reality I had been living up until then did not match the supposed reality being portrayed in the media. My experience and my instincts told me that the French-speaking people of Quebec were not terrorists. It was not until my peers saw me approaching and would say to me "Here comes the terrorist"; or heard me speak French and would shout out "Speak White!", that I began to grasp the reality that being a French speaker singled me out as a terrorist in the minds of English-speaking Canadians.

Speaking French with my family had become a dangerous act. The shaming, humiliating effects of the accusations hurled at me led me to distance myself from my francophone roots and culture. My world felt extremely unsafe. I stopped speaking French that year. My need to fit in had become stronger than my need to claim my difference.

How does a person heal from the shaming tactics used for generations to subdue and assimilate people? You turn to your ancestors for inspiration. That person, for me, was my Mémère, my paternal grandmother, Germaine Tétrault.

Mémère, born and raised in Quebec, was forced to emigrate to Saskatchewan with her husband in the early 1920s to escape poverty and establish a farm on which they could raise their four children. During the first forty years, she lived in Glentworth – a tiny farming community where less than five percent of the population spoke French. For the last twenty years of her life, she lived with her daughter and son-in-law, Lawrence, who only spoke English. I often witnessed conversations between her and my uncle where she would address him in French, and he would address her in English. I wondered why she never spoke English, and he never spoke French.

I'll never forget the time shortly before Mémère died. She was in the Regina Hospital 300 miles from her home. I was in my mid-twenties at the time. Every day after work, I would head to the hospital to comfort her as she lay dying. Given the medical staff's inability to speak French, I was quickly called upon to translate. I felt like such a failure! My decision to stop speaking French ten years earlier had left me able to understand Mémère, but I struggled to find the words to convey information from the hospital staff. It was even more difficult to speak to Mémère from my heart.

It was that encounter with Mémère that changed the course of my life. I will never know why she did not speak English – was it a form of protest at having been forced to leave her homeland? Was it an act of resistance to those who would have admonished her to "Speak White" or labeled her as a "terrorist"? I will never know. What I do know is that she inspired me to recognize the importance of language as a critical part of personal identity.

Her resolve to speak her mother tongue gave me the resolve to seek work that would take me to Quebec, thus enabling me to regain my mother tongue and to claim my rightful heritage as Fransaskoise – a person of Francophone heritage born in Saskatchewan. It would enable me to be employed as a French Immersion teacher of students in the public school system, teaching them to speak French and instilling in them a sense of appreciation for French culture and language.

Mémère helped me to reclaim my difference and to tell the stories of those silenced by the words "Speak White" and "Here comes the terrorist." For your courage and your inspiration - Merçi, Mémère!

***

Lise Tétrault is Fransaskoise – a person of Francophone heritage born in Saskatchewan, Canada. An Educator at heart, she has a deep sense of curiosity for how things work and what makes people "tick." Lise is a perpetual seeker of her French/First Nation Métis heritage, an aspiring storyteller, and a self-proclaimed doodle artist.

17

The Broken Places

by Kristi Cromwell

M y dad died… twice. The first time wasn't a real death, but as a young girl, my dad's leaving was the first real crossroad in my life. It would take me a few years before I was able to talk about the void his absence left.

Before he died, life was filled with joyful days and trips to the Eastern Shore of Maryland to visit dad's parents, my grandfather and my step-grandmother. They had a cottage on the water, and my sister and I were allowed to go out in the weathered rowboat with dad and grandfather. We were fashionable in our one-piece swimsuits and fuzzy slippers. I remember crisply made beds and sheer curtains that billowed in the afternoon breeze.

I was born in Michigan, but our family lived mostly in Virginia. We moved for a short time to Binghamton, New York, where my dad was to complete training for his new job at IBM. It wasn't long after we arrived that he decided the training wasn't for him, and we moved back to the Washington, D.C., area. That might have been a foreshadowing that he gave up on things easily.

My dad was an engineer of sorts. He got a job at NASA Goddard Space Flight Center in Maryland. My sister and I were allowed to visit once and saw some of the projects that he worked on. There was a lot of shiny metal and large computer reels. It was exciting that my dad worked at such an important place. Proudly, I took a framed black and white picture of a rocket to my preschool class for show and tell.

I wish there were more memories of these times, but there aren't. My parents divorced when I was about four years old, and my world fell apart. I maybe saw him once after that, when he took my sister and me by train to the New York World's Fair. My young life was disrupted, and my sense of security and self-worth began to crumble.

Perhaps you had a similar beginning, too. Your compass gets broken, and you wobble your way through the years trying to find your own sense of direction.

My mom, my sister Kathi, and I then moved to another city in Virginia, where I would attend Kindergarten and first grade. We somehow adjusted to our new life, but something was missing. We lived in a townhouse and one of my fondest memories of summer during that time was listening to the Whippoorwill sing its song in the muggy night air as it drifted in through the open window. The rhythmic song was a comfort to me during an uncertain time.

My sister and I joined the Majorettes. She led the older girls in the parades, and I led the younger girls. What a team we were in our white outfits trimmed in blue and our white boots with blue tassels.

I gained a bit of confidence, but my heart was still broken. Life went on, and it was just the three of us… at least, for a while. My mom started dating, and it was another turning point when we found out that she would remarry. We would be moving yet again to another new town.

I started my second-grade year in a new place, leaving old friends and places behind. I found it increasingly difficult to talk about my family, not really understanding what had happened or why I never saw my dad. At the beginning of the school year, when students and teachers ask questions about each other's families, I found it easier to say that my dad had died. Because, in my heart, he had. I didn't know how else to process it or to explain his absence.

I continued to wonder about my dad as I got older. Did he ever care about me? Where did he live? Was he remarried? Why didn't he love me? It was awkward on Father's Day to see the cards in the drugstore that I couldn't buy. It was awkward when my doctors would ask about the medical background on my dad's side of the family and I knew nothing. All these questions continued to haunt me, and the answers never came.

Sometimes the unknown answers push us to grow in ways we never knew we could. We become resilient, we build character, and we become self-reliant... if we're lucky.

Years passed. Feelings of abandonment lingered. Feelings of low self-worth lingered too. My need to know grew, and I wanted to put the pieces of my life's puzzle together.

I did some detective work and was finally able to locate my dad through a distant relative when I was twenty-nine years old. I found a phone number and I dialed it. I was told to wait for him to call me. I waited anxiously for that call, and it came about a week later. Strange voice on the other end of the line. Strange feeling in my heart.

We met shortly after that in the lobby of a local hotel. He brought me flowers. I told him I didn't know whether to hug him or hit him. Anger was simmering. Years of stuffing away feelings started to unravel... and then feelings of gratitude for being reunited started to surface.

When I found him, we were living only an hour apart. I had lived in the same area for five years, and ironically, I would be moving to another state in a month's time. I found out that I had three half-siblings. More pieces from my childhood found, but also lost. It wasn't the warm and fuzzy reunion I thought it would be... we were different... things were still awkward... phone calls were sporadic... bits of advice were shared... and there was an occasional "I love you." We both had blue eyes, though. He was my father, after all.

Resolution started to happen, even though there was still a hole in my heart and in my spirit that couldn't conceivably be filled. Life made things complicated. Distance made things complicated.

Colon cancer made things even more complicated. I was at his bedside at the end, as were my siblings and even my mother, his first wife.

I reflected on how I was there for him in ways he was never able to be there for me. It hurt for a bit, but then… it was okay. Sometimes it's the healing of the broken places that makes us whole again.

As my dad was dying a second time, things came full circle. In the early morning hours, we softly played his favorite music as he was passing. Tears fell from his eyes. We all took turns saying our goodbyes. I held his hand. I told him I loved him one more time, and that I forgave him for his absence. He had loved me in his own way, he did the best he knew how, and that had to be enough.

***

Kristi Cromwell is a writer and photographer. In her former career as a speech-language pathologist, she enjoyed helping others find their voice and communicate more effectively. As a Guided Autobiography facilitator, she now helps people find purpose through memoir writing. Kristi sees writing and photography as important tools for healing. She lives with her family in a beautiful hollow in Massachusetts.

18

On Turning Sixty in Corporate America
by Jan Dunham

F or much of my twenties, I reveled in being the youngest person in my corner of the corporate world. I was as fresh-faced and naive as a newborn, if newborns sported voluminous 80s perms, L'eggs Sheer Energy Suntan Pantyhose, and floppy silk neckties.

I envied my older colleagues' experience and mastery of office politics, but couldn't imagine being so *old*. Wrinkles, bifocals, retirement planning – it all pointed to a vaguely distasteful future too far in the future for me to imagine.

My, how the conference room tables have turned. On a continuum from bright young thing to crone, as I approach the age of sixty, I suspect my colleagues would place me closer to Dowager Countess of Grantham than Miss Jean in *The Prime of Miss Jean Brodie.*

Frankly, I could have used a heads-up. Why is there no handbook breaking down how you're going to break down? I'm convinced a *What To Expect When You're Decaying* or a *What Color Is Your Hair, Really?* would have eased the shock of the demon eyebrow furrow of my thirties, the surly chin whisker that took up residence in my forties, and the recent marionette lines that would give Pinocchio a run for his money.

For several years now, I've audited such tiny, relentless betrayals of my flesh with a powerful makeup mirror purchased after my close-up vision wandered off. While discovering a new wrinkle or age spot isn't the most self-affirming way to start your day, I can't deny that 10x magnification is queasily entertaining, like watching roadkill in extreme close-up.

The Mirror of Masochism callously reflects today's carnage, but it doesn't prepare me for what time and gravity have in store. For that, I rely on other women.

Not the women I see in the media, those TV anchors encased in bronzer and full-body shapewear, the actresses with plastic surgeons on speed dial. Women in their sixties and seventies from any TV show, movie, or *People Magazine* cover today look less like your grandma than your mom did in her forties.

Rather than rely on celebrities for a preview of coming subtractions, I look to the women around me. Pretending to listen to a coworker in a meeting, I furtively assess her crow's feet, and scrutinize the newly astonished expression of an executive "back from Greece." And naturally, I closely monitor the faces, necks, hands, and backsides of all of my friends, whether they're two months or twenty years older than me.

But as I close in on sixty, it's clear that *I've* become the office canary in the coal mine of decline. A younger coworker stares at my neck in rapt fascination during a staff meeting. Over the coffee break, the eyes of a fortyish colleague dart glances at my bare upper arms. I invest heavily in scarves, keep a jacket on standby, and complain loudly about the AC.

In the merciless glare of the overhead lights, I check the restroom mirror to make sure my lip fuzz is invisible and my gray hairs are fully camouflaged. I mull over teeth whitening, more frequent Botox, and whether highlights would make me look sun-kissed or desperate.

Get a grip, I tell myself. Find the sane and healthy line between aging gracefully and American Horror Story. Stop obsessing and put all this energy toward working on your *inner* beauty.

The problem with inner beauty, of course, is that it's invisible and fails to convey to one's coworkers or hiring managers that one is *keeping up,* that you know what Tik Tok is, and that you are all over the blessed news that high-waisted jeans are back.

In Corporate America, I'm convinced it's best for a woman not to exceed forty-five. If we're being honest, thirty-six is better, but a stylish mid-forties is acceptable – old enough to be experienced, but not old enough to be, you know, *old*.

Cross the Frightful Frontier of Fifty, however, and you'll encounter the unspoken expectation that you'll do everything in your power to not *remind* people about it. This becomes less a matter of vanity than economics, as layoff data and age discrimination lawsuits attest. Continued aging can put one's continued employment at risk, along with such handy perks as regular paychecks and healthcare benefits.

To ward off pity and pink slips, I gut my gray, freeze my forehead, and pummel my pores at considerable discomfort and greater expense. I bully into submission body parts my grandmothers wisely ignored. I pay sadists in Spandex to convince me that pain is in my best interest. I defer the selection of new glasses to a twenty-something with sleeve tattoos, who pronounces them "on fleek, totally the right casual note."

There's nothing casual about aging, given its role as a precursor to not existing. But it does have its silver linings (so much more elegant than "gray linings," am I right?).

A personal favorite is Ubiquivision, the pleasure of 24/7 eyesight that awaits after you give in and wear the glasses already. I'm also inordinately fond of Pain-Free Mobility, which comes with escaping the tyranny of pointy high heels.

Best of all is the Badass Brigade, older women who refuse to fade gracefully into the cubicle walls. They rock their unstructured jackets, proudly regard wrinkles as proof they're survivors, not that their idea of sunblock in their twenties was baby oil. They make noise and take up space.

I too will swap self-effacement for self-assurance. Instead of obsessing over slackening physical and mental capacities, I will cultivate self-knowledge and wisdom and mindfulness, like so much morally superior zucchini.

Boldly will I inform my colleagues: I'm not going anywhere. So stop asking me when I'm going to retire already.

I am your future.

On your path to sixty, you too will discover the relentless power of gravity and how too often people regard you differently as you age.

But, I will reassure them, there is compensation for the crow's feet, for that cloak of invisibility you don't remember putting on. As you wane, you'll gain. Quite a lot, it turns out.

Instead of measuring success by your employer's yardstick, you'll measure it by your values. You'll realize that your bottom line increasingly has little to do with cash flow.

Driving ambition may yield to slower, more scenic routes. Pursuing your passions might become more compelling than promotions. Settling for less, amazingly, turns out to be more.

I won't pretend that I always like what I see in that mirror (seriously, *another* mole?). But I am trying to spend less time gazing at my reflection and more time looking outward. To do a 10x better job of showing my gratitude for the people in my life.

To. Slow. Down.

To be more forgiving of mistakes and missteps, my own and others'. To embrace how loss sweetens all that remains. To measure my worth not by how well someone decides I'm doing my job, but by how well I'm living my life – my one beautiful, imperfect, miraculous life.

Like a good moisturizer, the deeper perspective that comes with age is your friend.

Fluorescent lights, however, are not.

***

A badge-carrying member of corporate America for many years, Jan Dunham most recently led employee communications for a large technology company. At various points, she was a freelance writer, full-time mother, and failed screenwriter. A certified Guided Autobiography instructor, she lives in Portland, Oregon.

19

After the Crash

by Sara Perry

After a sunny day at the beach, my friend Pam and I eased our sunburnt bodies into her two-seat sports car to return home. It was late May, 1977. A week earlier, I had arrived home in Bethesda, Maryland, for the summer. Only one more semester to earn my bachelor's degree in Communication at the University of Colorado in Boulder.

When I started to put my seat belt on, Pam rebuked me, saying I didn't trust her driving. Putting on seat belts back then was not routine like it is today. Not wanting to insult her, I did not fasten my seat belt.

I have worn a safety belt for every car ride since.

Five minutes from her home on a two-lane road, Pam fell asleep. I didn't realize it. Her car collided head-on with a car in the other lane. My torso slammed into the dashboard, followed a split second later by my face hitting and cracking the windshield, splitting the top of my left ear and cutting my forehead and mouth. Four people who were picnicking nearby witnessed the crash and ran to help.

Two ambulances rushed us to Suburban Hospital, where we were admitted to the Trauma Unit. After we were stitched up and stabilized, we were admitted to the hospital. I had cuts on my face where I had hit the windshield and I was badly bruised. For me, the worst pain was my very bruised ribs. It hurt to breathe.

The head-on collision was not the only crash. A ton of bricks crashed through the unconscious defenses that had successfully defended me from really comprehending that I would die someday, that I could die anytime. Our culture then, even more than today, avoided talking about death in many ways. I was one of many people well-defended against that reality.

One day I was a twenty-two-year-old with my whole life ahead of me. The next day I was a twenty-two-year-old whose every car ride, every day, every night, felt to be my last. The invisible noose tightening around my neck made its presence known to me in the daytime and chased me in my dreams at night.

This was it. I was going to die in my twenties. Young men and women in their twenties tend to think of themselves as invincible. We don't expect to die in our twenties. That changed dramatically for me the day of the car accident.

I'm still trying to find words to explain the unexplainable. Most people have not understood what I meant by experiencing the awareness of my mortality. They thought it was some kind of conscious and intellectual process that had occurred, that I had realized I could've died in the accident and so I was scared of dying. But it was much, much more than that. It wasn't something that occurred in my mind. It was something that occurred in my entire being.

The felt awareness of my death was like a tide. When the tide was in, the invisible noose tightened around my neck, and I very much felt the awareness of my mortality. When the tide was out, the awareness receded into the background of my conscious awareness. Not regular or predictable, like tides in nature are, these tides came and went in an unpredictable pattern. In the beginning, the tide was in most of the time. Now, forty-four years later, the tide rarely comes in.

I wanted to find out about people who knew they would die soon due to advanced illness. Did they have an experiential awareness of their mortality? I managed to find some first-hand accounts, and I watched documentaries. There were enough similarities in our experiences that I felt validated.

I didn't know it then, but this was the beginning of my path to becoming a hospice social worker. In a nutshell, a hospice social worker helps people within months, weeks, days, or hours of dying—and their families—to cope, adjust, make difficult decisions, prepare for what's next, and in other ways navigate what is a very challenging journey.

I wasn't ready then to step into the role of hospice counselor. Too many unhealed wounds. Too much anxiety. And not enough credentials. That wouldn't happen until I was thirty-one. Then, I was healed enough psychologically—and had the credentials—to be a counselor for hospice patients and their families.

How did the car accident forty-four years ago change my life? In the process of my trying to understand what I was experiencing after the crash, I discovered my vocation. At the time of the accident, I knew I wanted to become a counselor. But in the years after the crash, I learned I wanted to be a hospice counselor.

Could I have found my way to being a hospice social worker without the car accident? Possibly. But I wonder if I would have known without a doubt this was the right vocation for me, a knowing that stayed with me throughout my career.

Although at the time—and for years afterward—I couldn't imagine anything good coming from the experiential awareness of my mortality, I gradually discovered additional ways that it had benefited me. The feeling that I didn't have much time left poured fuel on the fire of needing to find healing for the many unhealed wounds that had somehow been released from their unconscious hiding places. Would I have the time—before I died young—to heal enough to step into the vocation that beckoned me?

Studying psychology and training in counseling helped me find some healing. But what helped most was facing and working through my issues through many years of counseling in my twenties, thirties, and forties. I wonder if I would have been as diligent about continuing to get the counseling I needed if I didn't have that felt sense that time was running out.

Because of all the psychological healing I had experienced, I developed a deep confidence in the healing process when working with patients. I believe that my knowing how much healing can happen in ordinary people came across non-verbally and added to their hope. Also, because I was not a stranger to psychological pain, I could calmly go as deep into someone's psychological pain as they were willing to go without needing to distance myself.

Of course, I would have preferred to grow in these ways without having a car accident. But given that the accident happened, I was able to find meaning in it based on the enduring benefits it led to in my life. The crash, dividing my life into before and after, was a very memorable crossroad in my life.

***

Sara Perry retired in 2017 from a long career in hospice social work. Hospice remains one of her passions, and she became a hospice volunteer after retiring. She is happily single, has a thirty-one-year-old son, and lives contentedly with her two Maine Coon cats in Maryland.

20

Thunderstruck

by Peggy Rosen

A sudden flash lights up the waning afternoon. Lightning hits the summit ridge with an explosive crack. A boom of thunder reverberates around the mountain.

"I felt that one in my legs!" Joe shouts from a ledge below me, his voice as sharp and jagged as the cliff's face.

I'm wedged into a narrow chimney of slick gray rock, my toes on a sloping nubbin. To keep from falling off this perch, I wrap my left arm around a stone lodged in the crevice at chest height.

"Alan!" I call out to my husband. He isn't far from me, but I can't hear him. The wind grabs our words and tosses them away into the void.

The two other climbers in our group, David and Janie, are somewhere above me.

Rain and tiny ice pellets needle my face and hands. It's summer, but snow swirls. I'm wet. I'm cold. And terrified.

I've never doubted that I'd get home from a climb. Until now.

Caught in the center of an unexpected storm high up on Middle Sister peak in the Rocky Mountains of Alberta, Canada, we need to get off the mountain.

The technical parts of our descent must be done one person at a time. It's slow going. I wait my turn to rappel down this section, only one of many rappels needed to retreat to safety. I shift my feet and try to control my trembling.

The peak shudders and hums with electric current from yet another nearby strike.

It occurs to me that metal attracts lightning. Steel gear dangles from my climbing harness.

After what seems an eternity of delay, it's finally time for me to rig the rope through my rappel device and clip in.

Before I begin to lower myself, exactly at the sound of the next crash of thunder, a jolt runs along the length of my arm.

That's the side my heart's on. This is it. I'm going to die right here from a lightning bolt.

But if I can think this thought, my heart hasn't stopped. I'm not dying. I can keep going, trying to get down.

Rope-length after rope-length, rappel after rappel, foot by foot, we make our way. Hours pass. It's not too much farther to the valley floor now. Rain falls and thunder rumbles, but with less intensity.

At the base of the mountain, we account for everybody. None of us is seriously injured, but we're not safe yet. Our crawl off the vertical crags has taken so long that night is folding in on us.

There's still a boulder field and scree slope to navigate and a stream to cross. In the dark.

My thoughts jump back to the previous evening at David and Janie's condo. While we readied our gear, David assured us that the climb wouldn't be difficult. If we traveled light and fast, we'd be home for lunch. He scoffed at the contents of the climbing packs that Alan, Joe, and I carried.

"You won't need all that stuff," he said.

David's "light and fast" approach to mountaineering got me worried. What if I couldn't keep up?

Feeling pressured by David and ignoring my own wisdom, I removed emergency gear from my pack to lighten my load for the next day's climb.

I might have gotten away with it. A lifetime ago, this morning, we'd hiked through dew-covered meadow grass in good spirits, looking

forward to a quick and satisfying morning ascent. The weather had
looked fine.

Now we're in pitch black wilderness, five people trying to find a path
through a jumble of mountain rubble by the light of only Alan's and Joe's
headlamps. Unlike me, they'd kept all their emergency gear in their
packs.

At least Alan, Joe, and I are wearing our standard mountaineering
apparel, the lightweight wool pants that retain some warmth when wet.
But Janie's in trouble. Her soaking wet cotton sweatpants contribute to
rapid heat loss and hypothermia. She stumbles and slurs her words. We
urge her forward, hoping that muscle movement will warm her and
prevent an even more critical drop in her core body temperature.

Boulders under our feet shift, move, and slide away to expose ankle-
breaking holes. Some of the dislodged rocks roll and bounce down the
slope. We need to stay close together, but it's easy to get separated as we
pick our way through the uneven landscape.

A thud on the back of my head makes me stagger. My ears ring. One
of our group unintentionally kicked a rock down. Thank God I'm still
wearing my climbing helmet.

I shake off a wave of dizziness and keep going.

Alan is holding Janie up by her elbow, helping her walk.

We find the stream, the last obstacle, and splash straight through it.
Getting wetter is hardly a concern at this point.

Finally, we reach the condo's front door. It's nearly midnight. I choke
on sobs of relief.

It takes hours for my racing heart to slow to its normal rate.

Over thirty years have gone by since that day. My Middle Sister
experience taught me to trust what I know—that emergency gear is
carried for the unexpected. I also learned something inherently more
valuable. I learned not to be intimidated, or to change my safety practices
because of being afraid of someone else's judgment or ridicule.

Today, as often happens now that I'm an "old" woman still active in
the outdoors, some young hikers pass me on the trail going up.

"Staying overnight?" one asks, nodding toward my loaded pack.

"No. Emergency gear."

They glance at each other, eyebrows raised, and continue. They carry small rucksacks and wear inadequate clothing and footwear for a trek above timberline in the White Mountains.

I want to stop them, tell them my Middle Sister story, about being prepared and trusting that preparation, about being smart in the mountains. But I don't. Like teenagers shrugging off a mother's advice, they wouldn't listen. I hope they aren't forced to learn a hard lesson someday.

The old helmet, sporting a jagged crack where a rock hit me in the head, still hangs in our gear closet to remind me of my own hard lesson learned long ago.

***

Peggy Rosen is a writer and certified Guided Autobiography instructor who uses small group workshops to help adults over fifty explore, write, and share their memories. She believes written personal stories can create powerful connections between people. Peggy writes, hikes, bikes, skis, and climbs in New Hampshire with her husband.

21

The Price of Understanding

by Paulette F. Stevens

A couple of years into my first marriage, I began to realize puzzling differences between my husband and me. We both loved being educators. We worked as teachers at a small private boarding school in the woods of Canterbury, New Hampshire. We enjoyed the students, had fun teaching, and liked living near his family in Massachusetts. The East has a different culture than the West, and it was an adventure for a western girl like me to integrate into this well-established New England community.

My husband's brother was married in 1970, just before we were. Riding in the car on the way to the church with some of his family members, I was surprised to hear an argument break out and wondered why the sons were so angry at their mother. I surmised that the animosity was connected to the fact that she was an alcoholic. Being naïve, I didn't know about this private grief from any personal experience, but the memory stuck.

My husband never talked about the frightening things that happened in their home with alcoholic parents. I soon realized that close relationships were challenging for him, and he was often unwilling to communicate with me. He seemed to be in emotional pain and pulled away into classical music, listening and spending long hours with his thoughts. If disturbed, he became irritated by my conversation and didn't want to hear about or discuss our children. I took on more responsibilities so as not to upset him, gave him space, and treated him kindly, anticipating that he would work things out on his own. But he didn't.

Years later, we moved west and settled in my hometown. He got a teaching position, and I cared for our seven children. As a family, we had some wonderful times, but the distance between my husband and me increased. I sensed his anger toward his mother had somehow been redirected toward me.

I looked for help to understand alcoholism and how it can affect someone who has never had a drop to drink. In a culture where the religion preaches "Word of Wisdom" and avoids drinking strong drinks of any kind, there wasn't much information or support available to me. I read books and learned that many children of alcoholic parents suffer from emotional issues as adults.

By this time, some rather dysfunctional patterns had been set, and the children began to treat me with disrespect as well. I didn't understand why, nor did I know how to defend myself. In a sort of darkness, we didn't talk, trust or feel. When my husband didn't want to communicate, he lifted a book or magazine between us to break eye contact. I felt hurt and discarded.

We needed an intervention, but he wouldn't think of going to a counselor. I remained true to the love I felt for my family, but nothing I did was good enough, and life with him was like walking on eggshells for me. When circumstances forced our hand, we found ourselves in a family therapy session with a counselor who explained why the patterns had gone so wrong. Afterward, she put her arm around my shoulder and said, "You have good guts."

On the way to the car, my oldest son asked, "Mom, why do you let Dad treat you like that?" I was stunned. The children had been aware of the situation all along, keenly watching me and my responses.

I looked into the mirror and saw a woman in emotional distress. I knew that if I didn't get out of the situation, my spirit would die, and my children would think this behavior was normal.

I filed for divorce in 1990. Our older children fled to the corners of their own worlds, hurt and angry with me, and I finished raising the younger ones without their father.

Two years later, I married a good, quiet man who loved me and was willing to accept my children in a broken state. One day, soon after our marriage, Don looked my belligerent daughter in the eye and spoke up on my behalf, firmly telling her, "You. Will. Not. Treat. My. Wife. That. Way. I love her." His words changed everything!

As a young mother, I did not know what I did not know, but I am grateful for the courage to get out of an abusive relationship and break the cycle of dysfunction. Eventually, we came out of the shadow of the effects of generational alcoholism, and my precious children and I continue to learn to talk, trust and feel in healthy ways again. What a price to pay for understanding!

***

Paulette Stevens is a former teacher, mother of seven, and co-founder of the Children's Museum of Utah. She has published over fifty books of personal history for her clients, and in 2012 established the Life Story Library Foundation to serve the global community. A visionary and humanitarian, she continues to collect, save and share the personal life stories of our time as valuable recorded history.

22

Tributaries of Life

by Leigh Morrow

M y life has been anything but typical. I moved five times before high school and another five times after University. I've lived in every geographical region of Canada except the far North. I've had three careers, two at the same time. I've seen sunrise with the saffron-robed monks of Laos and sunset in the hospice with my Dad. I've beaten the marriage odds and we are celebrating our 25th, with nothing silver except our hair, dancing with the Rolling Stones when they tour this May. That same month, I'm also entering my first half marathon. What the hell.

To use the river metaphor, there are many tributaries that have contributed to the blessed richness of my life. My river has deep channels, fast turbulent flows, and a rich sandy sediment bed.

It's impossible to rank the branching points of my life by which have been the most important, as all have carved me. But the loss of our twin girls at birth led to the deepest grief I had ever experienced.

I went from being a very pregnant first-time Mom, thrilled to be carrying twins, to a mostly silent, grieving woman with painfully engorged breasts, a cruel twist that only those that have lost newborns understand. I remember driving back from the crematorium, in my sports car, with my two babies' remains in small identical white cardboard boxes on the passenger seat.

I had planned to sell my car, thinking we all would not fit in my two-seat Miata, but here we were.

That February, I watched from my living room window the grass turn the most iridescent shades of green.

During my grief, I experienced the most intense colors I had ever seen. The view of my front yard is forever etched in my memory from those first few weeks without my girls, who we had named Celina and Natalie.

The hedge of heather along my driveway, the early shoots of new blades of grass, the hard rain as it hit my window pane and rolled down like my never-ending tears. Everything looked sharper, more focused. The intensity of colors is hard to explain to anyone who has not waded into the deep pool of grief. Sounds were magnified as well. I couldn't bear to hear the TV or the radio. I needed the house to be silent. I sat a lot and just stared out the window.

Like all my highs and lows, I wrote through them. I journaled, and we went to grief meetings with other couples who had lost a child.

It's a secret club that no one asks to join. For eight weeks, we sat around a big office table, with a box of Kleenex on each end. We told each other our painful stories, partly because no one else wanted to hear them.

I remember the most common comment I would receive after "Oh, I'm so sorry," was "Well, you'll just have to try again!"

Like I had tumbled off a horse.

Feeling so raw and exposed as grief gnaws its way through you, it's very difficult to volunteer for another pregnancy.

Yet I knew that the death of my girls had drawn an invisible but permanent line in the sand of my life.

If I did not try to have another baby, we would mark the events of our marriage on this tragic timeline.

A calendar whose only date was "before the girls" and "after the girls."

On April 24th of the following year, the skies opened up over my house, and it began to hail.

I smiled, thinking how appropriate that was, on my first day home with my one-week-old daughter Hailey.

She was a preemie, so small she looked like a baby bird that had fallen from the nest. I would hold her little neck with my thumb and my index finger to burp her.

Her skin was covered in downy fetal hair, and she wore the tiniest pair of sunglasses as she basked in the blue-lit neonatal tanning bed to treat her jaundice.

Against the rules of the maternity ward, I secretly breastfed her before the nurse would weigh her each morning in an effort to fill her tummy and cheat her weight up to the magic number of five pounds, so we could go home. I desperately wanted to go home.

Half baked, with old-man wrinkles instead of fat, her fingers and toes seemed disproportionately long, yet she would sleep like a yoga master, with her feet tucked up by her head, just as she did in my womb.

She seldom cried, content to slumber in flannel sheets I would swaddle around the two of us like a mama kangaroo.

To me, she was beyond beautiful, verging on remarkable, and on the rare occasion when she opened those big brown eyes, I was euphoric.

Out of the tributary of grief, heart-wrenching despair, and darkness, a new fork had emerged, a new stream born of hope and faith.

A new branching of my life, showing me that the deeper sorrow carves its channel, the more joy your river can hold.

***

For as long as she can remember, Leigh Morrow has been helping people tell their stories. As an investigative reporter for over twenty-seven years, both in radio and television, she has been privileged to hear and share so many important narratives. Now, as one of The Story Guides, she finds joy in helping others tell their stories through teaching Guided Autobiography in partnership with Lily Bengfort.

23

The Phoenix

by Hsu Shu Fen

I t's been over thirty years since the accident, but I still cry as I write
this. On the surface, I am brave. But my heart wants to pretend the
accident never happened. Writing about it in my Guided Autobiography
group, I remembered and felt once again the vulnerability and pain of
hidden suffering.

In 1988, after a year of training, I earned my paragliding certificate. I
fulfilled the dream of flying that I had carried since I was a child. One
day I was flying with a bird beside me. I could see the droplets from its
flapping wings. What an exhilarating experience!

The accident happened when I was thirty-two, a year after I earned my
certificate. On a very windy day, I went paragliding with friends at Green
Bay, in the northern part of Taiwan. I was excited to be the first one to
glide. The wind was so strong that day that the coach had to tie a rope to
my paragliding suit to prevent me from being dragged into the sea.
However, I was no match to the wind's powerful force.

I fell onto the beach from seventy-five feet up in the air, about the
height of a five-story building. As a nurse, I knew I was in danger.
Moments before I passed out, I told my friends, "Don't move me."

The hospital staff confirmed that I had suffered compression fractures
of the third and fourth vertebrae of my lumbar spine. I also had severe
abdominal distention; my intestines could not move because of nerve

compression. The surgeon told my parents that surgery was very risky, but they made the difficult decision to have it done.

The six-hour surgery went well, but the postoperative rehabilitation was long and painstaking. First, my body was put in a cast to prevent the displacement of the steel plates that locked my bones in place. After six weeks, the cast was removed and replaced with a full-body, steel-frame stent. I could not stand or sit for a long time. My muscles atrophied due to long periods without movement.

I never thought I could lie in bed, immobile, for so long. I kept telling myself, "It's a dream. When I wake up, I'll be back to where I used to be." But the torturous pain persisted one tomorrow after another. Everything seemed hopeless.

Thankfully, I had a group of friends who gave me reasons to be strong. My parents took good care of me. They never let on to their anxiety, but I knew they suffered no less than me. My father made me a chair so I could sit properly and comfortably.

During that time, a teacher wrote a postcard to me each week to encourage me. I wrote back, "God gave everyone a life, but he especially cares for me. He gave me two lives. One is running, jumping, and lively splashing. The other, the life of the future. Should I sit behind a desk, like an office worker?" It took me two days to write my response, and I realized that even with the pain and suffering, I did not need to waste my life grieving! I could choose to accept the pain and keep doing my daily work.

After two years, the steel frame was surgically removed. Many times, I would say to my body, "You hurt me, but I do my thing. We respect each other."

After all these years, my injured lumbar spine still causes pain and discomfort. I've changed my lifestyle to adapt to it, but sometimes I have unconscious reactions because of the accident. I often yell if my husband suddenly increases the speed of the car, for example. I quarrel with him as if the shadow of my high-speed fall is still in my mind. I'm afraid to watch any movie about "high falls" or "falling in the air." The fear of falling still has a space in my heart and has become a weakness of mine.

The process of writing my story helped me reflect on my fears. What am I afraid of losing? How should I face loss? When I first thought about it, my tears kept streaming, my heart raced, and my hands trembled. Repeated reflection made me see myself clearly again. With tears, I saw the brave, sunny, happy, cheerful, and active girl who went through so many painful events yet still retains her enthusiasm for life. Even filled with sadness and fear, I am also filled with love from the warmth and care of all the people who supported me during my rehabilitation.

"Who am I?" I am a person who is loved and able to love others. My fall turned out to be a step in a journey to an enriching life. Because of my experience, I can better understand the suffering of other patients. I know it may not be easy to overcome my fears, but with this love, I'm sure I can do it.

***

After graduating from the School of Nursing in 1977, Hsu Shu Fen worked in nursing for thirteen years. She was a long-term care facility Vice President twenty-three years, during which time she introduced nostalgic treatment to the clinical setting. In 2010, she earned her Master's in Information Management.

24

The Things You Can Control

by Carol Briam

A t the age of thirty-five, I quit my job and moved to Nigeria with my husband, Jean-Pierre, and our infant son. It was a year of change and challenges.

In 1989, everything seemed unreliable on the outskirts of Lagos, where we lived. Power outages occurred every day, requiring us to make regular use of a large, noisy generator for electricity. All our household water had to be delivered by truck to a tank and then filtered for drinking. Getting a dial tone on the telephone could take forever, and there was no guarantee a call would go through.

Security, though, was our biggest concern. Our house, like most expatriate houses nearby, had multiple reinforced doors and metal window barriers. Locking — or unlocking — everything took about twenty minutes and required a set of at least forty keys. Despite these precautions, we soon discovered they were not enough.

One night at 3 a.m., we awoke to the sound of intruders pounding with a sledgehammer. They had already hammered their way through an outside wall to gain entrance to the house, but our noisy generator had prevented us from hearing them. Now they were pounding their way through a second interior wall to bypass a reinforced door to a hallway leading to our bedroom.

Inside our bedroom, JP and I began preparing for the impending arrival of the intruders. I picked up a short-wave radio that I had never used and repeated a plea for help on each of the six channels, without knowing if any of my husband's German colleagues could hear me. At the same time, JP was listening through the bedroom door.

In our panicked state, we quickly agreed that he would open the door for the intruders once they were in the hallway. We believed they would be less agitated if they did not have to bust down the door.

Feeling vulnerable in my flannel nightgown, I wanted to change into a shirt and slacks. But my hands and legs were shaking uncontrollably, and I couldn't make them obey me. All I managed to do was slip on a pair of slacks under my nightgown.

I lifted our nine-month-old baby out of his crib, held him in my arms, and crouched into the bottom shelf of a wide closet. Although I was not hidden from view, I hoped that if the attackers came in shooting, any initial spray of bullets would miss the baby and me.

The dreaded moment came: the intruders were in the hallway. JP opened the door.

About fifteen men, armed with handguns, swept into our bedroom. A handful of them held JP at gunpoint and started leading him away.

Time froze for a moment as I looked at my husband. I wondered if this would be the last time I would see him. But I told myself that I had to put JP out of my mind. I could not worry about his well-being because I had to focus on keeping the baby and me safe and getting us through this ordeal.

The room was full of men. One of them groped me while others swept through the bedroom, overturning the mattress and rummaging through dresser drawers in search of money and jewelry.

Somehow, I recalled the security training I had received a few years previously on dealing with mob violence. Two key points from the training came to me:

• *Speak to one person only, not multiple people.* Doing this focuses the mob's attention on the interaction between two people, which is better than having the mob focused on a single, potential victim.

- *Speak in an assertive tone, but not an aggressive tone.* Even if a person is not in a position of power, acting as if one has power can influence the perception and actions of others.

Something in my sub-conscience kicked in, and I began using what I had learned in training. I directed my attention to one of the robbers: "Take what you want and get out," I ordered.

At one point, the robber grabbed hold of my son's arm and began pulling him away from me. I immediately removed his hand from the baby and said sternly, "You don't touch him." He did not touch the baby again.

The robbers swarmed through the entire house. After what seemed like an eternity, the police finally arrived, prompting the robbers to flee through the backyard with their loot.

Arriving at the same time as the police were two of JP's colleagues, relieved to find us safe. Having heard my plea on the radio, the colleagues rushed to the police station and paid cash to entice the police to come help us.

With the robbers gone, the police left soon after.

The sun rose, and, bizarrely, everything seemed "normal" again. I prepared the baby's bottle and put on a pot of coffee for the colleagues seated in our living room.

That evening, we moved temporarily into a hotel. By day, we worked to get our house back in order and repair the gaping holes in the walls.

But another hole remained that needed repairing — a hole in my soul.

Soon after the robbery, while with a friend, I began feeling overwhelmingly nervous and jittery for no apparent reason. I wasn't myself. Being a bundle of nerves was not me, and I knew I had to do something.

The remedy was clear to me: I needed to channel my thinking and efforts into something I loved. And something I loved was the new field of desktop publishing.

As a former newspaper reporter, I had become enthralled with the revolutionary technologies that made it possible for a single person to magically design and produce documents with beautiful typography and images, avoiding manual typesetting and massive printing presses.

I scoured computer magazines and researched the products I would need: an Apple Macintosh computer, a laser printer, a handheld scanner, page layout software, electrical transformers, surge protectors … and, importantly, many manuals and books as there was no support nearby.

I dipped into savings and placed the orders. Shipped by sea from the U.S., the products took a few months to arrive.

It was a momentous day when the boxes arrived, I remember the joy of opening them and unpacking my supplies. In a room where a gaping hole had been repaired, I set up my study. My beloved books and equipment filled the empty space.

I spent hours exploring this wonderful technology I now had at my fingertips. I dove into all sorts of desktop publishing projects for myself and others.

My study became my sanctuary, and my passion became my lifeline out of the quagmire. I regained a sense of calm, as well as profound satisfaction.

By the grace of God, my family and I survived a distressing attack. By the same grace, I thrived in the aftermath.

***

Carol Briam, Ph.D., of Saint Petersburg, Florida, has taught non-fiction writing and business communication at universities in France and Dubai. She first became interested in Life Story in her twenties while writing obituaries for a newspaper in Arizona. Today she enjoys helping people write their extraordinary and everyday life stories.

PART 2 | Choices

Choices are the hinges of destiny.

— Edwin Markham

25

What a Ruined Manicure Taught Me About Life
by Lisa Culhane

L ife's funny, but not always in a fit of giggles kind of way. As I sat sipping coffee on the porch in the cool of that spring morning, my life had felt the wrong kind of funny for almost a year.

First, my life had been stirred and then vigorously shaken. The experience had left me wandering in that uncomfortable hinterland between the death of life as I knew it and the birth of something new.

I had ended up in what I, as a Life Coach, call "Square One."

Square One is no man's land, when life as you know it ceases to exist but you haven't yet metamorphized into your next incarnation. Much like a caterpillar who has spun a cocoon and dissolved into bug soup before re-encoding its DNA into its new form as a butterfly, Square One is a place best described as "goo."

If you've ever been through a major life transition, perhaps you can relate.

Over the previous nine months, seemingly unrelated events had changed the way I viewed my country, myself, and my life. I had retreated into my own personal cocoon, turning into goo while doing the bare minimum life required, reassuring my fragile self, trying to trust that the goo of my life would somehow rebuild itself into an incarnation that I felt comfortable inhabiting.

Thus, when I realized that I wanted to start a project, I was thrilled. It was the first hint of Square Two peeking out. This phase always follows

Square One but usually arrives much slower than we desire. It is often so long in coming that it can feel like rain on drought-parched earth. It's the phase where we start to reimagine our life.

The project that called to me seemed easy enough. As I sat drinking my coffee, I stared at one tiny corner of the garden that needed a good weeding. After so many months of neglect, there was much that needed doing around the house and in the yard. I was looking for something manageable, and this corner of the garden fit the bill.

I was no more than ten minutes into my weeding project when my gardening gloves came off, proving far too cumbersome for the exacting task of separating the ground cover from the vine-like weeds.

An hour or so later, I sat back, contemplating my ruined manicure and my incessant internal monologue. I began to giggle as I realized that I had unwittingly chosen a project that mirrored my life of the past nine months.

I first noted that this was a much more difficult task than I initially imagined. I then noticed that when pulling the things I didn't want, I had to be careful to leave the things I did want. Sometimes the two were so entwined I couldn't get to the roots and had to settle for just taking out the part I could easily see and deal with.

Other times I was able to dig deeper and extract the root. However, I still didn't know if I had gotten the whole thing or if there was more I couldn't see or feel deeper underground. And throughout the process, I knew that some of the weeds would grow back, and it would be my responsibility to get to them quicker next time before they overshadowed the things I wanted to keep and nurture.

In the first hour or so of weeding, my wandering stream of consciousness had covered, in no particular order: denying the actual complexity and size of the task, resisting taking on the responsibility, anger that I was the one responsible for such a thankless job, bargaining with myself about how I deserved to be rewarded for such selfless and valiant behavior, and resentment that others weren't doing more.

Finally, my mind got around to having the conversation with itself about how it was my choice to spend time weeding the garden. How, at any time, I could make a different choice. I could be the person who weeds the garden or not, as long as I was at peace with my decision.

And it was those wonderings that led to a feeling of acceptance, peace, and even joy in completing my weeding project. I get how hyperbolic this sounds – a weeded garden hardly counts as life-changing. But for me, on that day, weeding felt analogous to my life.

The weeds tangled together with the established plants reflected the incongruent feelings of loss and pride I felt as my daughter left the nest, moving over a thousand miles away to start college. It mirrored the struggle, sadness, and satisfaction I had faced as the primary caregiver for my mom while she negotiated the space between a pancreatic cancer diagnosis and death. It reflected the frustration and determination I felt when our nation elected a leader I despised. It reminded me of the complexity of saying a final goodbye to my mom and reconciling all the tangled feelings we have for the imperfect humans who parent us.

The weeding also brought to mind the apprehension and the joy I felt as an imperfect parent sending my own daughter out into the world. It reminded me of the periodic happiness and validation I had experienced as a caregiver for my mom, especially when I focused on my ability to choose what I wanted to do, how I wanted to do it, and who I wanted to be in the process, rather than dwelling on the day-to-day tedium and inevitable outcome.

Those weeds reminded me of my own responsibility to advocate for a world purged of sexist, racist, homophobic, xenophobic, and religious bigotry.

That one tiny corner of the garden, on that particular day, was a reminder that it's always appropriate to giggle, even when – perhaps especially when – we feel like goo. The simplest things can help us find more meaning and strength in life's endings, transitions, and new beginnings.

***

Lisa Culhane is a Life and Legacy Strategist, Certified Life Coach, author, Guided Autobiography Instructor and compulsive traveler who spent a year traveling the world with her family. In her spare time, Lisa is a reading tutor, avid hiker, Tarot Card dabbler, and personal assistant to her rather spoiled dog.

26

Back to the World

by Marie Rowe

J ust before Christmas 1971, my friend Pat and I hit the road with our backpacks to escape our mundane au pair work in Zurich. Lacking in funds and with no real direction, we headed for St. Moritz, where we spent a magical Christmas. This was mainly thanks to the kindness of a stranger, an American GI who encouraged my friend and me to head for Stuttgart and the 5th General American Army Hospital where we could find work. This path, albeit circuitous, was the beginning of a whole new chapter in both our lives.

We showed our passports to the skinny, freckle-faced young soldier on the gate of the 5th General and asked if he would direct us to the personnel office.

"New blood?" he said.

"Yes, we might be giving blood," I answered. He gave me a puzzled look, and Pat giggled.

Pat, a nurse, had her interview first while I sat on a chair outside the personnel office, nervously waiting. She emerged with a smile on her face. "I'm in!"

"What do you do, ma'am?" the rather robust personnel lady in a tight-fitting army uniform asked me. "I'm a secretary," I replied. "Great! They need a secretary in the lab to run the drug abuse program." And that was pretty much it. I was in too!

We were given accommodations in the civilian quarters of the hospital and, after obtaining the necessary work permits, we were soon immersed in the somewhat "M*A*S*H" atmosphere of this very un-traditional hospital.

Pat was assigned to what was called "the drug ward" on the third floor, while I was taken to an office in the laboratory on the second floor of the four-story, white-washed building. I shared this office with my boss, Sergeant Friedlander, who was funny without knowing it and was the very image of the TV character Sergeant Bilko. My other office mate was a female, Captain Cartwright, who was not too fond of men. She was very intimidating, with a bulldog attitude, and was Sergeant Friedlander's nemesis.

The lab was a reflection of the relaxed attitude of the military workers, who seemed to be merely passing the time as they completed their tours of duty. Blood Bank, Pathology, and Urinalysis were some of the departments just a few doors down from my office, and rock music played constantly. It was a fun atmosphere.

My first day on the job, a chubby GI in fatigues and John Lennon glasses arrived in my office carrying a large, black plastic bag slung over his shoulder – like a misplaced Santa Claus.

"Are you the drug lady, ma'am?" he looked at me with a hopeful expression. I think I nodded, and then he dropped the bag on my desk. Small plastic bottles of various honey shades of liquid rolled out.

As I looked at the mountain of urine-filled plastic bottles on my desk, Sergeant Friedlander peered over his horn-rimmed glasses and said, "Time to get to work. See, they're all labeled with the name and unit." He went on to explain that there were several American army bases in the Stuttgart area, and all military personnel had to supply urine samples.

Drug addiction was a real problem with American soldiers fighting the war in Vietnam, especially as time went on and there seemed to be no end to the conflict. If they weren't drug-addicted before they were drafted, as many were, they soon began to rely on drugs to tolerate the horrors of a war they often knew little about. Marijuana was common and easily attainable in Vietnam, but when these young, vulnerable soldiers were arrested for using this particular drug, they began reaching for harder drugs such as heroin, opium, and LSD, in order to cope with their brutal situation. These drugs were less detectable, but much more addictive and damaging.

The kind and patient Sergeant Friedlander handed me a notebook and explained that I needed to log all names and serial numbers and then send the bottles off to a lab in Landstuhl, where the samples were tested for "illicit" drugs. When there were positive results, I'd tell Sergeant Friedlander, who contacted the relevant army unit, and the soldiers were then hospitalized on the drug ward.

These heroin-addicted soldiers spent two weeks on the ward to "clean up their act." Two weeks to become drug-free! Even though I wasn't particularly savvy about drug addiction, common sense told me that it took a lot longer than fourteen days to kick the habit.

Every day, the addicts came down to the lab to submit their urine samples. Some of them were in various stages of drug withdrawal, and it was painful to see them in such distress. Each soldier had to be supervised as they peed into a plastic bottle. Thankfully, that wasn't part of my job! But it was for Sergeant Friedlander. He was too embarrassed to stand watching each soldier, so he looked away, which gave the GI's an opportunity to substitute someone else's urine. I later learned that an orderly on the drug ward who often accompanied the soldiers into the lab was not only providing the addicts with his urine but also supplying them with the drugs they needed. For a price, naturally.

Consequently, the drug abuse program, which had recently been implemented by President Nixon in an effort to deal with the drug problem and rehabilitate soldiers returning from Vietnam, was a complete farce and an exercise in futility.

One of the GI's, Daryl, who worked in Hematology, was tall and lanky and walked as if he had springs in his shoes. He literally bounced everywhere. One day he bounced up behind me and yelled right in my ear, "I'm short! I'm short!" Clearly, this didn't refer to his height but meant that soon his tour of duty would be over. He had a short time left in Germany, and then he would be going home. "Back to the world!" This is what the soldiers called America. To them, America was the world. So many of them, even though they were in Europe, had no interest in exploring other countries. They would often just stay in the Stuttgart area for the two years they were stationed at the hospital or the bases nearby. I thought how wonderful that they loved their country so much, that it was the world to them. Pretty ironic, when you think about it. Soldiers who'd fought in Vietnam were often shunned when they went "back to the world" and didn't have the hero's welcome awarded soldiers from previous wars. They were treated like disposables.

As an English girl being thrown into a somewhat dysfunctional situation like this, you'd think I'd want to get as far away as possible from these crazy Yanks. But that wasn't the case at all. Regardless of the problems I was made aware of, I was very fond of these diverse Americans and appreciated their openness and generosity of spirit, as well as their "can-do" attitude. That's when I made my decision to move to America, where many more wonderful adventures awaited me.

***

English born Marie Rowe spent thirty years in the Hollywood film industry as a writer, casting director, publicist, producer, and actress. She worked primarily with writer/director Barry Levinson on most of his films, including "Good Morning, Vietnam" and "Rain Man." She now gives inspirational talks based on her Hollywood experiences.

27

A Path Reaffirmed

by Steve Hoover

There are crossroads in life that offer trajectories and potentialities—new directions, possibilities, and promises. And then there are intersecting paths, coming at a time of personal and professional crisis, which re-affirm life's purpose.

My life and Richard's intersected briefly and intensely, beginning in the fall of 1979. Entering my third year of teaching and my first year at Suncoast Middle School, I was in the midst of the challenges and disillusionment many new teachers face. Too many students, little support, and limited income create the educational trifecta that leads fifty percent of new teachers to leave the profession in the first three years. I had left Indiana on a whim to escape a backwater town and a dead-end teaching job. Unfortunately, sun and sand did little to brighten the underlying issues of a job that seemed less than a career.

I first met Richard and his parents at school orientation the week before classes began. Parents and students moved from room to room, listening to an overview of the curriculum, viewing their classrooms, and meeting their new teachers. As Richard was in my homeroom and first-period class, he and his parents came to my room first and arrived early —a habit I would soon recognize as a survival strategy. Initially, their early arrival irritated me as I was caught up in the preparations necessary for meeting 120 students and their parents. Nevertheless, if one is fortunate and alert, there are crystallizing moments when our lives intersect with someone's hopes and dreams, giving us the opportunity to grow. Such a moment came for me when Richard's parents handed me a brochure on sickle-cell anemia and asked that I look it over and call them if I had any questions. Then they thanked me and quietly took seats at the back of the room, by the door, where Richard would spend his time in my classroom all year.

So often, teachers become inured to the parents who inject themselves into our lives. They advocate aggressively for their child and, consequently, alienate other parents and us. This was clearly not the case for Richard's parents. Theirs was a simple request to merely read a pre-printed flyer, one I could have ignored amidst the chaos that was my life.

Richard was one of the smallest students in my eighth-grade physical science class in a newly integrated middle school in North Fort Myers, Florida. He was one of many African American children who daily rode one of seven buses from the Dunbar area, one of the poorest and crime-ridden sections of town, to the redneck center of central Florida. Bus ramp and hallway fights were a regular occurrence, and a diminutive, chronically-ill student was a potential target. On days when Richard could attend school, he made it his habit to come immediately to my first-period classroom to avoid the threats of hallways and lockers—sometimes carrying all his books in an overloaded backpack. The stress of physical violence, long, noisy bus rides, and carrying a forty-pound load constantly threatened and often succeeded in triggering episodes of his sickle-cell anemia.

I learned a little about sickle-cell anemia from that flyer and a little more from the school nurse. However, my real education came not from books, pamphlets, or health-care professionals but from Richard, his parents, and his brothers and sisters. I learned about his dream to become a doctor and find a cure for his disease, both for himself and other children. He desperately wanted to graduate from high school but knew he was falling behind due to how challenging it was for him to manage the long bus ride and a full day of school. He was afraid he wouldn't even graduate eighth grade.

Richard taught me first-hand what a sickle-cell crisis looks like—and feels like. I saw what it was like for him to navigate a system that marginalizes a condition for which there is little hope and implicit bias. I also learned that sometimes a teacher's job is not limited to the content of the classroom, it extends to the relationships we have with our students' hopes and dreams and the content of their character.

When Richard was too tired to navigate a day in school, I learned about his hopes and dreams at his hospital bedside and at his home. I saw how his family supported his hopes and dreams even though they understood the reality of his illness. I laughed as Richard told me jokes he'd heard on the bus, which I was asked to never share with his mother. He would ask me about college and if it was hard, and if I thought he was smart enough to go there and graduate. Sometimes, when he was sicker than usual, I would collect his homework from the other teachers on the team and send it on the bus. That night, we would talk briefly on the phone, although his mother generally intervened as he tired. When I offered suggestions on how to help him with his math or science homework, she would chuckle and hand the phone to her husband.

Richard did make it to high school. His parents and family, along with my co-teachers, made sure that he mastered what was needed to graduate middle school. However, the demands of the high school curriculum, his progressive condition, and the inability of the educational system to adapt to his needs made his eighth-grade graduation his last.

I have stayed in teaching for over forty-five years. Even in retirement, I teach senior citizens health-promotion and Guided Autobiography.

Richard's was one of so many of my life's memorable intersections, but it came at a time of professional crisis when I needed shoring up. I have been deeply in Richard's debt for these many years, and I am so very grateful that I chose the path on which we met and never diverged from it.

***

Steve Hoover retired from St. Cloud State University in 2018 after having prepared hundreds of teachers over a twenty-nine-year career. Prior to that, he taught physical and biological sciences to middle and high school students. After failing to fully retire, he is now the Healthy Aging Coordinator for the Central Minnesota Council on Aging.

28

Morning Press

by Reneé B. Johnson

That morning, I rolled out of bed smack into a crossroads.
Usually, I get up and head downstairs with the clothes for the day over my arm and don't come back upstairs until bedtime. But my daughter was off at camp for the summer, so I had the run of the upstairs bathroom and the leisure to linger in my bedroom.

Looking out from the crisp sheets with the sense of the possibilities that an open calendar provides, I realized that over the last few weeks, clutter had accumulated here as in other parts of my home.

An article I once read suggested a simplified decor made for better sleep, the idea being that your mind wouldn't have as many things to work on to keep you awake. Or was it the voice of my daddy saying, "Everything has a place and everything in its place" that had prompted me to keep my room neat and uncluttered? I'm not sure if the article was right, but I did find the orderly minimalism very pleasant, creating a bit of an oasis in my room. Other than my clothes folded in color order on open shelving, my collection of bells, the ironing board, and the rocking chair I rarely sat in, there wasn't much else to divert one's attention from sleep.

That morning though, there was stuff on every horizontal surface! There was laundry half put-away; summer sandals in a heap; various articles of clothing hung from hat box strings and shelving; an errant scarf on the floor near the vacuum cleaner brought up weeks ago for a deep cleaning; the rocker out of place; and, underneath it all, the carpet in need of yet another deep vacuuming. The morning was cool enough to make working upstairs agreeable, so "why not?" I asked myself.

Why not, indeed? A quick run through the morning necessities across the hall, and I was back in my room, assessing the damage and mapping a plan of attack. No point vacuuming until things are picked up. I can't put the laundry away until the clothes hanging from the shelves are put away. Bingo! Re-hang clothes in the closet! That's the place to start. Yea, but these are summer-weight clothes, and there are more mixed into the other closet. So maybe it is switch-the-season time for my two small closets. Is there room enough to do so? Will it make sense just by season? Is there a better configuration? Is there enough room? Do pants go with dresses or dresses with skirts? Organize by size or season or color?

All those questions were why my closets have never been seasonal or better organized. There is too much to consider, too much to do. More aptly referred to as "clothes presses," in the historical sense of the word, both closets were chock full. One held hanged and bagged clothes I can no longer wear but cherish and hold out hope of one day fitting into again. The other was packed with the clothes that fit but most of which I don't ever wear. Just because they fit your body doesn't mean they fit you. Easier to leave the presses as is than to answer those questions, expend that energy, and make decisions regarding the left or the right. I'd been down that road before and still hadn't found the answers.

Some years ago, I divested my clothes presses of the beautiful wool suits that had become impractical in global-warming southern Illinois and my more casual work life. The linens and silks remained, as did a couple of significant wool pieces, pieces that at one time defined my professional persona and still speak to me of the strength and accomplishments of that woman. Also among the special items were those that my mother had tailor-made for me. There was the umber-colored raw silk jacket that perfectly set off the flowing two-piece jacquard silk dress I first wore to Ann and Lawrence's wedding; the many-gored skirt and matching shirt in earth-toned rayon that was scandalously above my knees in length; the royal blue raw silk suit that made me stand tall and regal at a conference in Canada. Perhaps it was time to remove these vestiges of another era, savoring the memories of that other me.

Lug out. Fold. Sort. Remember. Repeat.

Repeat until there is a yawning emptiness with just my daughter's handmade High School Graduation dress remaining, imitating the white of the walls and ceiling. No time for Mama's pride reminiscing now. Onward, to fill the closet with . . .? Pants! Yes, pants in order by length, color, and weight on identical pant hangers. Ah, the perfect symmetry; no longer a simple press. Reordered tops and dresses in the other closet; hangers spread two-fingers-width apart. Symmetry once again!

I had a sense of calm readiness, perched on my bed, looking into both closets. There just might be something to this "calm your room, calm your life" thing. Without a glance in any direction, I strolled out of my oasis, satisfied that I had achieved a herculean feat taking myself forward into a state of closet nirvana.

Gentle readers, the glow of my closets had blinded me to the reality that I was still in the crux of the crossroad moment. With piles of sized and folded clothes now littering the floor; discarded hangers piled here and there on clean laundry; Goodwill donations thrown in the rocking chair still out of place; and now, more than one errant scarf blocking the path to the vacuum, the clutter remained and had grown! Isn't that just like a point of departure! You're giddy with excitement for the adventure ahead, and for a moment, the realities of your life fade into insignificance.

A week later, my closets glow with order and calm. They are pleasant companions to my morning routine, clearly showing me the choices for each occasion. However, to reach either closet, I must step over or skootch around the detritus of that glorious morning. That morning when I thought, "Why not?" Why not become a person who didn't hoard old clothes, who accepted today's size and cleared clutter to make room for new possibilities and deeper sleep?

Habit? Fear? Surely, I could let go of these lovely bits of fabric assembled just so, but could I let go of the person who wore them or the way they made me feel? Would I ever again feel that inner wonderment at my fierceness?

Of course, I would. And I have, and I do. It's not just the clothes; it's me.

So it is time to bag and box these pretties and move them on to another. Without hesitation, I am ready for the day's task. Perhaps these bits of fabric, now devoid of my expectations, will find their way to a woman who needs just a little nudge toward wonderment. I hope so.

***

Reneé Johnson is a woman of curiosity and creativity eager to learn and share. She was the mentor for and author of the 2019 children's book project, Alton ABC. *Professionally, she consults with non-profit organizations on many issues and assists library patrons as they delve into their family history.*

29

Skiing My Way to a New Life
by Michele Halseide

Too steep.

That's what I told myself, peering down a narrow mountain trail now snow-packed and groomed for cross-country skiing. I knew how to snowplow and turn on downhill skis, but on cross-country skis, I lacked control, like an eighteen-wheeler with failing brakes. I knew what would happen when my downhill speed exceeded my comfort level. I pictured the outcome: me sprawled at the bottom. Or, worse yet, me skiing off the edge, crashing into trees, and somersaulting down jagged slopes. Not pretty.

My knees began to shake.

"I can't do this," I told my husband, Phil, an expert skier. Our weekend retreat to Lone Mountain Ranch outside Big Sky, Montana, was supposed to be relaxing. Most cross-country trails are flat golf courses in the summer. But not this one. This trail was for telemark skiers, not novices like me who intensely dislike speed.

Phil offered a solution.

"Come around behind me and put your skis inside of mine," he suggested, assuming a spread-eagle position. "Now, put your hands around my waist and hold on."

I side-stepped into position and got behind Phil. Then he pushed off with both poles.

To my great relief, his strategy worked. Phil's strong legs and skillful turns kept us safe. We made it down Lone Mountain, hill after hill, though I never could see the path ahead. I was skiing blind, so to speak, trusting Phil to make the turns and slow us down as necessary. A few times, when the grade steepened yet more, I closed my eyes. I couldn't look!

Then I heard an inner voice speak to me: *This is how it's going to be for a while. Get behind your husband.*

I was happy to do that—on Lone Mountain, anyway. I wanted to ski between his skis and hang on to him over every jarring bump.

But off that mountain, I was anything but weak-kneed. For decades, I'd plowed ahead in life, often independently, on numerous business ventures, building projects, and educational endeavors. For example, I'd opened Roosters, a gift store and coffee house in Sheridan, Wyoming, nearly fifteen years earlier. I'd designed and managed house remodels, land purchases, and the building of our Big Horn home. I'd written for publications, rarely asking for Phil's feedback. I'd even founded and directed a school for accelerated learning. All pretty much on my own.

So being told to *get behind my husband* sounded odd to me, like a foreign language. No chance this was my imagination speaking! This subtle command had to be God's idea. But how far would He take it?

Looking back, I see "crossroad" written all over this Montana getaway, a gift from our kids. They wanted us to "start living again," after years of working six days a week. For months, we'd agonized over renewing our now-expired lease for Roosters. A thirty-day notice loomed over us, but we could not commit to five more years.

I was fifty-seven at the time, weary from the financial stress and long hours Roosters required. My legs throbbed in pain after standing at the service counter all day. I simply could not envision running our busy store much longer. Maybe a few more years? But not ten, or even five. Maybe just long enough to find a buyer. Finally, on our way to Lone Mountain, the landlord called for an answer. "Would you consider three years?" he asked. I reluctantly said yes.

So that Monday, after returning from Montana, I reviewed the proposed three-year lease and requested a few changes. By Friday, a final legal document sat on my desk: Black ink on white paper, ready for my signature and Phil's, as he was also a managing member of our LLC.

Admittedly, I was tempted to forge his signature as wives often do for their husbands and simply fax it back that day. *Get 'er done. Make it happen.* But I stopped myself. Get behind your husband echoed through my spirit. *All right, all right, I'll get him to sign it for himself.*

I stuffed the lease into my briefcase and headed home to find Phil sitting before his computer, perusing properties in Montana on Realtor.com. "Look at this," he said with enthusiasm, clicking on photos of a secluded mountain home. "We can sell our current house," he proposed, "and replace it with something comparable outside Bozeman —for half the price! Then we'd have money to travel or do whatever we want, and you wouldn't have to work, period."

I liked that idea. And I loved his newfound enthusiasm. I had not seen Phil so excited about anything, let alone real estate, in years. I was the one who was always flipping through real estate magazines. Equally shocking, my technology-challenged husband had actually figured out how to set up an account and password at Realtor.com! I was speechless. And then he dropped the bomb.

"I don't think we should sign that lease," he said, staring bold-faced into my eyes. My heart fell to my feet. "Really?" I questioned. *How can Phil make such a life-changing decision so fast?* I wondered. I'd spent months praying for direction, researching alternatives, looking for a buyer. Could I trust this impulse that seemed so out-of-character for my cautious husband?

Think of it: After just a few hours of research and deliberation, he was ready to give up both the business and home I'd painstakingly designed and built over several decades. Easy for him, right? Harder for me! My identity was entangled in both.

And then I remembered our ski trip. I heard those words again: *Get behind your husband.*

Until then, I had welcomed new adventures, never fearing change. But with Phil turning sixty-five in a few years, I had assumed we'd hunker down in Big Horn and grow old surrounded by long-time friends. *Why the sudden change in course now?* I pictured us at the helm of a huge ship, trying to change course abruptly. It wouldn't be easy.

However, thanks to that voice on Lone Mountain, tearing up the three-year lease seemed like the obvious thing to do—like discarding sour milk. Who would debate that decision? So that's what I did; I got behind my husband and prayed for more time to find a buyer. Six months later, she appeared unsolicited. A few years after that, our Big Horn property would finally sell, allowing us to move wherever God led.

Today we live in Westcliffe, Colorado—not Montana—where we hike almost daily in the Sangre de Cristo Mountains. Our lifestyle here is a dream come true. But that's not all. I no longer carry the weight of decisions and commitments made as a couple—at my insistence—in our 30s, 40s, and 50s. I no longer feel responsible for my husband's happiness—or lack thereof. That's a relief, honestly, like removing a heavy backpack. Like the exhilaration of skiing down Lone Mountain behind Phil. Now I'm free to enjoy the ride without fear, regret, or second-guessing.

And, to no surprise, I love where his turns have taken us.

***

Michele Halseide has spent the last four decades storytelling and writing for ad agencies, businesses, publications, and radio programs. She also ran an inspiration bookstore and coffeehouse for fifteen years before discovering Guided Autobiography. Michele blogs and teaches Writing Your Soul Stories online from her Colorado home.

30

Of Goats and Guinea Pigs

by Linda J. Schmidt

"Does that smell funny?" I turned to my lab partner in time to save my eyebrows. The fumes that escaped the flask drifted over the blue flame of the Bunsen burner, and the air glowed and dimmed with uncanny fire. What had we done? What was I doing there? My passion was words, not chemicals. The cute boy I had for a lab partner was as clueless as I was. Our experiment went up in flames with a puff of gas.

Months earlier, I had pored over the course catalog in my dorm room, searching for a suitable major. I loved to read and write but was too practical to major in English. As my granddad used to say, "Let's be practical." Instead of buying a new car, he would save his money and then be up to his elbows under the hood of his old car, tinkering with his tools to get it running again. My grandmother loved to fish, but he was the one who cleaned her lake perch so we could eat them for supper. I guess I got it from him, a practical streak that ran so deep that my dreams couldn't pry it loose.

I chose to major in biology and chemistry so that I could get a job out of college, not imagining how I could support myself with an English degree. I was told to dream big by my teachers, so I dreamed of becoming an author with a pile of published books. I dreamed on paper in my journals, dreamed of the characters as I read book after book.

But I was also intrigued by the diversity of nature, the patterns, fascinated by the endless ways that chemicals combined. I only doubted my major when my freshman honors English professor wrote "Excellent writing, you could've passed out of this class" at the top of my first paper. I remember closing my chemistry book in frustration as the beauty of what I had seen during a chemistry experiment was reduced to Xs, Ys, and pieces of the periodic table. Life reduced to symbols plonked into equations. So, I had written my paper instead, fingers flying, imagination fired, my love for words pouring out on the paper.

I got my biology degree with a chemistry minor and walked off campus into a research lab. I loved the people, and I loved the quiet whirring of equipment and the sound of printers churning out graphs after I fed data into my calculator. But what was I doing? The lab was in the federal animal research lab, my boss a brilliant Dutch lady named Louisa, whom I loved and admired. But we were studying a cow disease. I like healthy beef, yes, but a cow disease consumed most of my time? It all became so abstract and so detached from my reality. I wanted out. My dreams were being crushed under endless lab results.

And I had to kill the guinea pigs. I had to kill the guinea pigs! They trusted me as I gently pierced their tender bellies and performed tests on them. After we got the results, an endless parade of numbers marched drearily across my calculator, and I had to kill the guinea pigs who had served their purpose. A fellow lab tech showed me his preferred way. He dumped them into a garbage can with dry ice and slammed on the lid as they were fumigated. I quickly found what I thought to be a more humane method. But I still had to kill the guinea pigs.

One day, Louisa stopped me as I was walking down the hall and asked me to go bleed the goat. That definitely was not in my job description. I donned huge white overalls so the goat stench would not permeate my clothing and gathered up some rubber stoppered tubes and a large syringe. A new challenge, I had to think of it that way. Or run the other way.

Outside was a small pasture. The goat was munching grass fifty feet away. I sidled up to the gray, grizzled animal, weeds trailing from his mouth, soulful eyes fixed on my face. I talked gently to him as he sized me up. His purpose in life at the lab was to create antibodies to the cow disease we were studying. We needed blood, goat blood, to test for levels. I quickly swung my leg over his back, grabbed his horns, and tilted his head back. Before he could react, I felt for the jugular, plunged the syringe, and blood spurted into my tubes. Mission accomplished, I swung my leg off his back and bolted to the fence. The goat was not happy, but I avoided the impact of horns on my backside.

I finally extricated myself from that lab, said goodbye to Louisa and the goat, and moved to a new city with my new husband. I worked in other labs, met more good people, but I felt like I was being snuffed out. Didn't I once have dreams?

That session with the course catalog, my choice of a science major, sent me down a path away from my passion. If I had chosen English or Journalism, honed my craft of writing, would I have had the chance to live in a way that was true to who I was, how I was created? I see now that studying science opened up my world to new knowledge and ideas. I was still being true to myself, my passion was just being ignited in new ways. Would I have written stories about goats and guinea pigs without that experience? Didn't I also have a passion for science?

With the gift of hindsight, I realized that writers need life experience and that lab work provided a myriad of stories for my writing. I increased my passion for science. I learned to cut the words that no longer served their purpose – a practice that writers call "killing your darlings," which is much easier than killing guinea pigs! I learned to research and applied that skill to the stories I wrote. My writing benefited from the people skills and work ethic that I acquired at the lab as well.

The lab stories line up like the flasks along my chemistry bench, memories waiting to be dressed up on their way to my blank page.

***

Linda J. Schmidt lives in Iowa with her husband. She is a mother of three and doting Nana of eight grandchildren – all of whom are above average and very cute. Linda teaches life story writing classes and helps families create personal history books.

31

The Untrodden Path Forward

by Concepcion D. Famatid

M y life's transition points have a penchant for drama. Viewing them from an older perspective, I can deduce lessons in life, new self-understanding, and funny encounters.

I'll start with a story about a joke I made to a person, which became a joke on me.

He was a colleague of my four older sisters. I was the kid sister to who he said "hi" each time he came around to visit them. Then came the day when my sisters were no longer home to entertain him because they were married or employed outside the city, and I was forced to talk to him.

I really was joking when I innocently asked him, "Why not get married?"

We were on our porch, and he was telling me how lonely he was at home without his mother, who was abroad visiting his sister's family in Singapore. I did not have an inkling he was interested in me.

To my big surprise, the weekend following that joking interlude, he arrived at my house with his mother and uncle trailing behind. He had already talked to my parents, and they agreed to this meeting. My parents might have thought he was the right guy for me in comparison to the two other gentlemen who were hoping to sweep me off my feet.

My innocent joke to him had turned back on me. I had to make a big decision.

He became my husband. I never, ever thought I would march to the altar with him two months later. My life changed there and then.

The lesson I learned here was: Never joke on matters like marriage, especially to a marriageable male.

I was a city girl all my life before marriage. When I transferred to the hinterland rural community to live with my husband and teach, every one of my friends in the city was surprised no end. But this new life was not a problem for me. In contrast to what my friends thought, I adjusted pretty well. I loved nature and had a peaceful life. In fact, I found rural life enjoyable. Funny encounters with local kids ensued one day concerning the local dialect (rural dialect called "karay-a"), involving words that I understood differently.

"We need water," I told my grade-six students in Home Economics. "We need to cook vegetables for snacks." One of them said, "May tubig sa bayong, Ma'am" (There is water in the bayong, Ma'am). I looked around and could not find any "bayong," for, in my mind, a bayong is an earthen jar or buri bag we use at the market to carry things.

"Where?" I asked again. "Dyan sa ba-id, Ma'am," said another student. This worsened my problem because in my city language, "ba-id" means to sharpen a knife on a whetstone. The student was actually telling me that the bayong was in the corner of the room.

What the heck was this? Their dialect was so perplexing to me! I finally got it when they pointed to the object. The "bayong" they were referring to was a five-meter-long, hollow bamboo pole, open at the top and closed at the bottom, which people used to fetch water from the well down the hillside spring. "Ba-id" to them was a location in the room.

Another funny encounter happened this way.

The one creature I detest most is the house lizard. One morning, while in front of my students, I felt something jump on me from the blackboard behind me. I felt it crawling on my back and thought it was an insect. But when I saw the tail of a lizard and felt its cold body, I shouted, "Tiki! Tiki!" in fear. I was jumping crazily, flailing my arms. My students were wondering why I was shouting "tiki, tiki," because to them, "tiki" describes a short or extra-small person in size, as when they say "ka tiki kanimo" (you are very small).

My students all stood up and curiously came to my side. They bent down to find a poor lizard on the floor, to which they said laughingly, "Ay, suk-suk gali!" (Its only a lizard!)

Now they understood that, to me, "tiki" meant lizard, which in their dialect was "suk-suk." What a disparity! In my city language, "suk-suk" meant to put on clothes!

Life is never perfect anywhere one goes. My rural life was no exception. There were beautiful, light moments as well as some difficult and unpleasant experiences, but these gave me precious life learning, lessons I did not know I needed. I came out surprisingly mature, with more self-confidence, wider perspectives, and a huge desire to do better in life economically. I was thankful for the change in environment from the one where I grew up. The lesson I got here was: don't be scared to venture into new paths or experiences because untrodden paths provide learning.

More doors opened to me after my stint in rural life.

Before each door, unexpected little dramas occurred. The first was when I suddenly resigned from my teaching position after six years in the hinterland community. The news became the talk of the town. When I applied and was hired as executive director of the Community Chest, I was called for training at the Development Academy of the Philippines in Manila. The head of my school district refused to release me, hence my resignation. My lesson: don't allow anybody to take away your chance to grow in another field of endeavor. As a trained executive director, I was confident I would acquire more self-improvement and better serve humanity.

I believe I was right to resign and take on new tasks, bigger responsibilities, and new acquaintances head-on in a new setting. My new office involved people belonging to the higher echelon of society in a region-wide community. I pleased important individuals with my exemplary performances as executive director of the Community Chest.

After a time, I received an invitation to apply and was hired as the regional Public Relations Officer of the Cottage Industry Development Office. Moreover, my exposure as a speaker to various audiences earned me invitations to teach college students part-time. This I accepted happily. From then on, I was a college teacher.

The upturns and downturns of my life's crossroads until I retired as a university professor could fill a book. The main lesson I learned from these dramatic episodes is: do not miss the opportunity to do a good deed for a person in need, next door, or in your community. Your goodness will return to you beautifully in life's crossroads ahead.

***

Concepcion D. Famatid is a retired Social Science professor and former Associate Dean of the College of Arts and Sciences at West Visayas State University, where she earned her Doctorate of Education in Educational Management. Today, she is a researcher, grant writer, and teacher of Guided Autobiography.

32

Moment of Truth

by Nancy Wick

I came into work one morning, sat down, and had to grit my teeth to keep from crying. I shook my head. *What's wrong with me?* It was a perfectly ordinary morning. Nothing had happened. Why was I so upset?

It was 1975, and I was working at my first real job out of college. I had a degree in Speech and Drama, but there weren't a lot of jobs in that field, so I'd gotten myself hired at a hospital, teaching supervisory training courses for employees. It was a job I was unsuited to in almost every way possible.

Start with the fact that I was quite a bit younger than most of the people in the classes. What did I have to teach them about communication that they didn't already know from their own experience? Then too, I didn't really know how to teach and felt really uncomfortable standing in front of a roomful of students, most of whom were not there voluntarily. They were sent by their managers.

Beyond the classes, there was another problem. A hospital is a highly structured, hierarchical environment—one that I understood not at all. For example, in a hospital, doctors are the top dogs and always get their way. So when I scheduled one of my classes in a conference room that one of the doctors was accustomed to using for his students, here's what happened: my students and I arrived at the door to find him and his students already there. When I told him I'd scheduled the room, the doctor walked out into the hall where I was standing, then jerked his thumb to indicate I should follow him as he walked off. He said not a word until we got to the office where conference rooms were scheduled.

"My class is in the usual conference room," he said to the secretary there. "This lady seems to think her class is scheduled for the room."

The secretary, who was a friend of mine, smiled at the doctor. "I'm sure we can work something out," she said. "You go back to your class."

When he was gone, I said, "I scheduled a class in there. He hadn't reserved the room."

She shook her head. "Doesn't matter. He's the doctor."

Another time, I brought in a small plastic oval with dried flowers pressed inside of it and hung it in the window of my office door. Shortly thereafter, I received a notice that the decoration needed to be taken down. Only regulation signs were allowed.

In both cases, I was furious. I felt that the rigid hierarchy gave way too much power to the doctors, and the strict rules didn't allow for even the slightest expression of individuality. But when I complained to my friends, they said that the job sounded interesting, that all jobs had their problems and I should just put up with the eccentricities of this one. So I plodded on, faithfully showing up at the appointed hour to do what I'd been hired to do. But I wasn't happy.

Then, after three-and-a-half years, came the day I walked in, sat down at my desk, and felt like crying. That got my attention. Something wasn't right. I began to think about what I could do about it.

First of all, I had to admit that I'd gotten myself into this mess. Studying theater because I was interested in it was all very well, but I knew it wasn't a very practical major, especially since I didn't want to teach. Then there was the fact that I'd uprooted myself from Kansas City, where I went to live after graduation, to this much smaller city in order to be with a man I'd become involved with in graduate school. Now he was out of the picture, and I was stuck. I had to make my own living somehow.

For a few months, I soldiered on, talking to friends about my unhappiness and fantasizing about going back to school or just moving away. Finally, I had the idea that I should ask for an unpaid leave of absence in order to give myself a chance to think about things. Being that it was summer, when we didn't offer classes, it seemed my boss could do without me for a while. I was able to negotiate four free weeks.

The first day off the job felt like an escape from prison. I rode my bike, visited my friends, gloried in relief. Shortly thereafter, I went off to my college town, where an old friend was going to graduate school and would let me stay with her. It felt strange to be on campus again, walking the paths I'd walked for six years of my life. The place I might have picked up that coveted journalism degree, which had been my original plan, but didn't. I gravitated to the bookstore, where I wandered the aisles, picking up random books that looked interesting.

That's where I found *What Color is Your Parachute?* by Richard Nelson Bolles. Beneath the quizzical title, the subtitle spoke directly to me: *A Practical Manual for Job-Hunters and Career-Changers*. I bought it immediately, then walked down the block to the Student Union and plopped down at one of the tables where I had studied as a student. I looked around. Soaring ceilings, marble walls, double tables with lamps that accommodated two people facing each other. And opposite the room was a candy counter where you could always pick up a Snickers Bar if you needed a break. I had always preferred this place to the library.

Now I began reading the book and came to the first exercise, which was to write your autobiography. I pulled out a spiral notebook I'd picked up in the bookstore and started to write. I wound up spending the rest of the day there, writing steadily. By the time I returned home a few days later, I'd completed the autobiography and had moved on to other exercises. I felt more excited about my life than I had in years.

As I worked through the book, I felt as if a fog was lifting, allowing me to see clearly. My answers to every question in the exercises seemed to lead to an inevitable conclusion: that whatever my next job was, it had to include writing. I also saw, just as clearly, that I couldn't go back to my old job. Yes, it would be safer to continue to work there while I looked for something else, but the mere thought of returning made me feel like I was carrying a backpack full of rocks. So I rejected the cautious route. I resigned from my position, signed up for temporary work, and began the job hunt.

It took me a year, but ultimately I convinced the editor of the town's daily newspaper to take a chance on me. It was the beginning of a thirty-five-year career in journalism. The experience taught me something I've used ever since: to always trust my gut. Deep down, I know what's right for me, and if I follow that guidance, I can't go wrong.

***

Nancy Wick wrote and edited for many years at the University of Washington in Seattle. Now retired, she writes personal essays and other nonfiction. She also enjoys volunteering and being active in the beautiful Northwest. Her work has appeared in Minerva Rising, Persimmon Tree, Summerset Review, *and* Longridge Review, *among others.*

33

Shifting Sands

by Robin Lynn Brooks

I am on a beach at King's Range in Northern California. The eastern edge of the dunes slopes up to land so rugged, coastal Route 1 is forced to move thirty-five miles inland.

It is 1980. I am twenty-seven. I am walking north along the water on a beautiful day—the sand white, the sky blue and cloudless.

Rock formations swell to boulders here and there on the beach, making good shelter at night or blessed shade at high noon.

I can see that the hills above me grow into higher hills in the distance, even low mountains. Sparse vegetation, mostly scrub, populates what's visible from here, as well as long grasses the color of faded gold this time of year, September.

On my feet, I wear inexpensive white sneakers—just thin canvas—the old-fashioned kind we wore as kids. I so want to feel the earth beneath my feet, bend my toes around things if I want to, like wearing ballet slippers.

I carry The North Face pack I bought at the seconds store in Berkeley, saving up for months working as a maid in Mendocino. I got a sleeping bag there, too, along with kits I sewed for a mountain parka and down vest. I found a pup tent for $7.99 at the local hardware store—orange and red—just big enough for my pack, sleeping bag, and me.

I am backpacking alone for the first time. I have come here to check out my gear. Do a trial run. I haven't done this before, so I figure this will be something simple, just hike along the beach a few days, sleep under the stars like I did last night, the formations of rock rising up from the sand offering the illusion of protection.

Yesterday I traveled about fourteen miles. I know this because my landlord in Elk (just south of Mendocino) loaned me an old topographic map, and I am charting my way. Most of the streams marked have long since dried up, or maybe it's just the wrong season. But I see evidence of where they ran.

I'm surprised to find that I'm not frightened. It seems like the most natural thing in the world to be here, backpacking alone, and so far, I'm excited. I love being alone. I had no idea.

I follow the beach. Most of the time, I look out at the ocean. I watch the horizon, that single line that never fluctuates, where sky meets sea. As I move along the shore, that line is always there, that seamless peace. No gap. No break. Just the comfort of all being right with the world when the earth is in communion with the sky.

I feel the foundation of that union, taking in that solid connection of earth and sky, a completeness, an undercurrent of balance, something to steady that part of me reeling from the events of the past year.

As I walk along the beach, the horizon line drawing me on, I think about how I have walked away from my husband and home and job in New England. And I am walking away from my mother, from the shadow of my father who died last year, from my twin sister, and from everyone else in my family. I am walking away from everything I have ever known, from a life in which I don't know who I am and within which I have no place.

I stop and take off my shoes and socks. I want to feel the sand between my toes. Tying my shoes and socks to my pack, I hoist it up again. I attach the strap at my waist and tighten those on either side of my chest. I like the way this feels, a sense of security as if my pack is hugging me. I step forward, and it feels good to move my body.

Reaching the water's edge, I wriggle my toes in the wet sand and then wade into the cool water. I am in the undertow, but the waves are mostly spent by the time they reach me. Still, a light pressure caresses my ankles and lower calves as the broken waves touch me.

Gulls fly and swirl up above, screeching out their lonely cries. Now and then, one spies a crab scuttling along the beach and dives suddenly to grasp it in its beak. Then, flying high, the gull drops the crab onto the rocks below, the shell bursting to offer up its sweet flesh.

The quiet thunder of the ocean fills my body. The smell of seaweed and salt. My being is immersed in the sheer pleasure and realness of sand and sea and sun.

I stand mesmerized as the waves crash and then slide into shore. I feel the rhythm of the water as it curls around my ankles and shins, pushing at my legs, seeking to pull me into its depths. Pushing, pulling, a slow dance filled with power, and I am caught in its rhythm. As I sink deeper and deeper into its primal movement, my senses remind me of another time, another rhythm that tickles my memory. But the memory doesn't surface. It is lost somewhere within me, buried too deep.

As if waking from a dream, I move out of the waves back onto sand darkened by the water. Nothing has changed. The sand is still here. The sea. The occasional boulders and that steady line of the horizon.

But, looking back at this line again, somehow it is no longer enough. I have lost that sense of peace.

I turn to look at the hill that rises from the beach and feel the unknown of it pulling me toward it. I feel it scratching at me to join it. I haven't brought hiking boots. All I have are these thin canvas sneaks. I find myself stirring, away from the water, toward the hill.

Stopping at a low rock to put shoes and socks back on, I set off to climb away from the here that I know and toward whatever it is I have yet to discover.

***

Robin Lynn Brooks is a published poet and playwright with an MFA in Sculpture from The School of the Museum on Fine Arts in Boston. She has published her own poetic memoir, The Blooming of the Lotus: a spiritual journey from trauma into light. *This essay is an excerpt from Robin's forthcoming memoir* IMPRINT: Earth, My Mother. Sky, My Father. *Robin lives in rural western Massachusetts.*

34

Going Home

by Mimm Patterson

I ran away from home in October 1991, when I was thirty-three years old.

I'd been planning my escape for years. First as a child with an active imagination in rural Pennsylvania, then with a brief marriage the summer of my sophomore year of college in Nebraska. I ran some more after graduating in 1980 with a degree in art and education. I climbed into Cici's silver Toyota Celica with my twelve-string guitar the same weekend that Mount Saint Helens erupted and rode shotgun all the way from Lincoln to Cici's parents' home in Sunnyvale, California.

In October 1991, when the hills above Berkeley exploded into flames, and because my running away was not yet complete, I called my mother. She and I spoke by phone every few weeks, but I hadn't been back to her trailer at Green Acres Mobile Home Park for a decade. She'd moved into the trailer twenty years earlier with her third husband, Earl, who had convinced her to sell the house where I had spent my childhood. Earl had disappeared from her life, but my mother still remained in the dark, nicotine tinged single-wide. During our conversation, while I spoke of the horrors of what was being lost in flames, and while the smoke from Berkeley drifted south and with it the ash from people's lives, I knew that, like Earl, it would not be long before I disappeared from her life, too.

At first, I simply stopped calling. Eventually, I sold all I owned and moved to Ireland.

It's easy to put physical distance between two objects. Two people. And I am good at that. I pretend to my friends in Donegal that I have no family. That she doesn't exist. Yet, despite the distance, I think of her often.

When you try to run away, you still carry everything with you. Suitcases and psychic wounds. Whole life experiences and fragments of the stories you tell yourself about the way things were.

It's the spring of 2010. I make a right-hand turn from Turkey Ridge Road onto the narrow circular drive. My mother stands in front of her trailer with a smile on her face and points to the place where I should park my rental.

She's tiny. She's dressed in jeans and a navy-blue mock turtleneck. Her hair, thinning and gray, is styled in the same shoulder-length, teased and lacquered bouffant I remember from when it was thick and Clairol red. Her false eyelashes are in place with just a touch of frosted shadow on the lids. Her lips are brick brown.

I have four days to reconnect with a woman I no longer know. Four days to learn she fell in love with a man she met speed dating at a bar in Fogelsville. Four days to discover she stopped drinking around the same time I left California for the Emerald Isle. Four days to explain why I left, and four days to find out why she never looked for me.

She spends the long weekend pulling out huge scrapbooks filled with family history. Pointing to uncles who died in the war, sharing yellowed newspaper clippings and notes written in her perfect Palmer penmanship.

I ask about my father. She lights up one of her Smoky Joe vanilla flavored cigars, exhales, and hands me a photograph with a quizzical look on her face.

"Why would you want to know about him?"

The photograph is black and white and as small as a matchbox. A man with an Air Force regulation buzz cut holds an infant. My father and me.

She takes another deep drag and asks again.

"Why would you want to know about him?"

Something is triggered in me, and I begin to sob. Between breaths, I say, "I'm trying to find out who I am."

She offers no comfort. No mothering embrace. Just a simple "oh." I half expect her to add, *is that all?*

I don't know why I decide to stay with her. Maybe I'm attempting to build a relationship. I want her to be the mother I needed when I was young. That doesn't happen. But I stay anyway. All the way to the end.

In 2019, in the middle of July, Pennsylvania experiences a massive heatwave. The air conditioning unit for my mother's trailer stops working. Her best friend Maryanne finds her naked and delirious, collapsed on the couch, with an internal temperature of 104 degrees. An ambulance is called. My mother never returns to the trailer she loves at Green Acres Mobile Home Park.

Diagnosed with moderate dementia and COPD, she is transferred to long-term care. The staff at Mosser Nursing Home love my mother. She's funny and patient, they say. She's nice to the nurses, and they laugh at her dirty jokes. She cries to go home. I'm the one to tell her she can't. She falls and has surgery for a broken hip. When she falls again, and the partial replacement fails, she's put through a second surgery.

It's clear she is failing. I visit as often as I can afford. But not as often as I should.

As my mother begins to forget her life, I begin to erase it. I pack up the trailer. Her few friends circle me like vultures. Maryanne gets the washer and dryer. Ronnie from next door, a piece of milk glass, David some furniture. I put my grandmother's writing desk, some bookshelves, and those three heavy scrapbooks in storage.

And then I go home.

We can never know for certain if the choices we make bring us closer to who we are meant to be. Sometimes I know that running away all those years ago was the wrong thing to do. Sometimes I know it saved my life.

***

Mimm Patterson is a yoga therapist, life coach, writer, and artist living in the San Francisco Bay Area. Her passion for supporting people's journeys toward a more creative engagement with life through movement, writing, and contemplative craft is infused with good humor and joy.

35

How I Became Lily and Ate Beef

by Lily Bengfort

I left New York City for Ames, Iowa, when I was sixteen years old.
Like many teenagers, I was searching for freedom. Freedom from the
restrictions placed on me as a young Indian woman. Freedom from the
restraints of my culture. Freedom from my mother, who tried to control
all aspects of our behavior by being a harsh disciplinarian. But most of
all, freedom from a home of sadness.

So, when my eldest brother Roop, the unofficial head of the family due
to my father's passing eighteen months earlier, said to me, "In New York,
I only see a bunch of unhappy people, and Iowa is a place that is nice and
has a relaxed atmosphere. Would you like to go with me to school in
Iowa?" I didn't hesitate.

Prior to my father's death, my mother would never have considered
such an option. But she was overwhelmed with being a widow and
supporting six children, so she readily agreed. She understood now that
she too could die and leave us orphans, and she wanted her children to be
a bit more independent (but not too much), and my brother provided the
means for more-but-not-too-much independence.

And so, I moved from New York City, where I had emigrated from
Guyana four years earlier, where I had graduated from high school. My
friends in high school knew me as Lilotama, my official name, and at
home, I went by "Camo," a family nickname.

When I arrived in Ames, Iowa, my brother introduced me to his roommates and all his friends. Unlike New York City, a city full of immigrants where people found my name easy to pronounce, these new friends could not pronounce my name. After many introductions and failed pronunciations, my brother simply said, "Just call her Lily." And so, a whole new life began for me in Iowa, where I became Lily, an English name signifying (ironically) a white flower.

I was raised Hindu. I had moved to the land of Iowa pork chops and beef, and I had never eaten either. My brother arranged housing for me with three Iowan women who were five or more years older than me. I was lonely and homesick, and they wanted to make life better for me. So, they made dinner every evening for the first two weeks. All consisted of either beef or pork and potatoes and vegetables. Every evening, I was no longer hungry. They were mystified. I could not tell them that I did not eat beef.

First, there's the "yuck factor." I had an aversion or disgust to these meats that many people feel towards the idea of eating insects, for example. But I wanted to honor their efforts, and after two weeks, I ate a little piece of beef. Thus, my diet changed. Accustomed to spiced and spicy foods, I learned to cook and eat lightly seasoned meat, potatoes, and vegetables.

Two of my roommates' dads were farmers. I could not understand why we always had to buy corn at the grocery store. It seemed ludicrous to me that they would not bring corn from home. Or why we couldn't get corn from friends in Iowa, where there are fields of corn as far as the eye can see. It was only later that I discovered that most of the corn grown in Iowa was for the animals and not for consumption by people.

A year later, I invited my roommates to visit me during summer break in New York City. My mother has prepared a special dish for them. It is not the spicy food she usually cooks because I have told her that their palates may not handle curry or spices. So, she has decided to bake fish with the lightest seasoning she can. It is delicious and not too spicy. My roommates are no longer hungry. They have eaten little. I discovered that they were grossed out by seeing a fish cooked whole with its head and tail on, accustomed as they are to filleted fish.

I lost a few things in Iowa. I lost the close connection to the traditions and culture of my immigrant community and family. I temporarily lost my Indo-Caribbean identity as I embraced my new American one. Our culture informs our identity, and it took me a while to fully embrace all the things I am. I lost whatever accent I had, although now, as I am older, old habits sometimes reassert themselves in my speech. I lost the ability to avert gazes and avoid pleasantries. I lost my fear of being robbed or harmed by others. I traded a cosmopolitan environment for one where I was different and stood out but didn't feel awkward about it.

I found a few things in Iowa. I found a husband and got married there. I found I had to check the weather and plan my life around it as the weather changes hour to hour. I gained a healthy fear for mother nature— cyclones, snowstorms, the kind of weather that fosters camaraderie. Not only did I have a new name from half of my family, I also found that our families were a lot alike. We loved to play cards. We loved to eat. We shared many of the same values.

The beauty of being in a mixed relationship is learning from your cultural differences and opening your eyes to a completely different perspective. I learned to play euchre and won over my new family members. I became accustomed to independent activities during family reunions. I learned to make "hot dishes" for my family and added them to my food repertoire. I learned to make potatoes for Iowans, and they learned to make rice for me. I learned to hurry up and eat lunch so that I could be hungry for dinner.

I also came out of Iowa different from what I had been before. The truly terrible loss of my father contributed a necessary foundation to my life's trajectory. It made my life more richly complex and catapulted me into un-imagined directions. It was expected that I would live at home until marriage. I left home at sixteen. It was expected that I would have an arranged marriage. I accepted the proposal of the one I wanted. It was expected that I would become a doctor. I switched to Journalism in college. In Iowa, I was exotic, in a sea of white flowers. In Guyana and my New York immigrant community, I was "lily-white" in a sea of exotic flowers.

No place is perfect, as I discovered at Iowa State University during the Iran Hostage Crisis when fifty-two Americans were held hostage. There were college demonstrations against Iran around the country with signage such as, "Deport all Iranians. Get the hell out of my country." During one of those demonstrations, I experienced real fear when I was mistaken for an Iranian. Then, and now, like many families, I must navigate not only cultural differences but also political divisions and prejudice. I sometimes joke with my husband that we could beat racism by playing cards together.

I am still Lilotama, but I am also Lily.

***

Lily Bengfort is a technology entrepreneur, Board Member of University and both for-profit and non-profit Boards. Lily finds joy in helping others write their stories as well as growing their businesses. She speaks and teaches business executives, educators, retirees, and those making life transitions. She is an advocate for creative aging and expanding entrepreneurial opportunities for women.

36

Summer of '86

by Heike Herma Thomsen

"**A**re you from Germany?" – a question that many Western German tourists did not really like to be asked when travelling the world in the 1980s. Following the motto "When in Rome," Germans tried to blend in with the surroundings when abroad, and mingling with other Germans was no part of this. So when the question was yelled at me across the room in this Vietnamese restaurant in the South of France, I was not too keen on answering.

I turned around somewhat grumpily and saw a young woman about my age grinning at me. Her black bob style perfectly matched the deep red lipstick she wore and gave her a classic yet dramatic look.

"Yes, I am," I answered curtly, hoping this would be enough to satisfy her interest, and went back to my conversation.

It was 1986, and I was a student spending a summer holiday with my Latin-American boyfriend, Diego, in France. We had decided to stay in Avignon for its annual festival because he expected to see many of his fellow musicians who were living in Paris there. At that time, Europe had become the destination for many Latin Americans to escape the political and economic unrest in their home countries.

We had decided to go on this trip after having lived through some very rough times as a couple, in particular since I had decided not to start a family with Diego. Even though it had been a painful experience, I felt it had been the right decision. Travelling to France with him might have been a subconscious way to test my emotions.

The atmosphere was lively and we had a very good time. Since I did not want everybody to understand what I was telling Diego, I sometimes switched to German – which the black-haired woman at the end of the long table had picked up. Turning back to my friends and continuing my conversation in Spanish did little to dissuade her and she continued, asking, "And where in Germany are you from?"

I really did not want to have a conversation with her, but I did not mean to be rude either, so I answered that I was from the north of Germany, close to Hamburg. Having said that, my manners kicked in, and I asked her in return where she was from.

"I am from Halle," she answered cheerfully. I was stunned. And a little confused because, even though I was not the grandmaster of German geography, I was pretty sure that Halle was a city in Eastern Germany and that it was not possible for her to be here if she had been from that city. However, I did not want to appear stupid either, so I just asked her:

"I'm sorry, did you say Halle? I know a Halle in Eastern Germany, but where are you from?"

"That is where I am from," she said in a slightly mocking tone.

The short answer game continued. But now, I was intrigued because she was from the German Democratic Republic and her presence here was a mystery to be solved.

"I thought that only retired people could travel outside the GDR," I said, sharing my wisdom on East German politics.

"Yes, that's true," she said.

She was not going to make this easy for me, so I asked directly, "Then tell me, how come you are here?"

"They kicked me out of the country," she answered. I finally stood up and took my chair to where she was sitting because now I was hooked and wanted to hear it all.

So Stella told me her incredible adventure of having a child with her Vietnamese boyfriend, which was not well seen in the German

Democratic Republic, and as a result, she was in the crosshairs of
surveillance by the Stasi – the state's security service. Fearing for her
safety, and in particular for losing her child, she married a Frenchman
who had come to the GDR with his political group and was later forced
to leave her country within twenty-four hours because of forbidden
Western contacts. She had ended up in Avignon with no money, no
French language skills, and no plan for the future, stealing fruit from the
fields, when our musician friends found her and took her in.

She did not want to go to Western Germany because she did not
connect herself with the people fleeing Eastern Germany or seeking
asylum. This did not really make sense to me, yet before I could tell her
that, Stella added, "If I knew a person in Western Germany with whom
we could stay for a while, I could start my new life," looking me directly
in the eye.

I understood the message loud and clear, and although I felt the
impulse to help, I was reluctant to invite her to the pathetic student
apartment that I shared with Diego. I wanted to be sure that I had the
facts right and considered the situation from all angles before I made a
massive decision.

Meanwhile, Diego had joined us and before you knew it, he had
leaned back in his chair, opened his arms, and said with a big smile, "Of
course, we are taking you with us. No problem!"

There he was again. Without a care in the world and without even
thinking about any consequences, he said what was on his mind. He
didn't even check with me because he knew I would be the one taking
care of everything as usual.

"You know, I think it is better if she is not coming with us. It is too
much responsibility," Diego told me a few hours later when reality had
slowly sunk into his brain, and he realised what it would mean to have a
woman and her confused five-year-old child living with us.

I was furious and told him that we could not back out of this decision
since we had provided her with the first light at the end of the tunnel in a
long time. "Whether you like it or not," I said, "they are now coming

with us," and at the moment I said it, I knew it was the right decision. I was sure I would be able to cope, and even felt a little proud of myself because it was a humane thing to do, and I felt good about it.

The next day we left for the North of Germany. Stella and her daughter spent six weeks in our tiny apartment until I had a nervous breakdown and asked her to move to her new apartment, which we had recently found, providing her with the essential furniture and things she needed. I felt badly, but I had reached my limits because, as expected, I had been alone in this.

Painful months followed until my relationship with Diego finally came to an end. Stella was my port in the storm during this time. I haven't heard from Diego since then. Stella, on the other hand, meanwhile a proud grandmother, has been a reliable fixture in my life for thirty-five years.

***

Heike Herma Thomsen holds an M.A. in English & Hispanic literature and is a Guided Autobiography Instructor, translator, and certified coach for Creative Writing and Poetry Therapy. In her thematic writing workshops, she guides people professionally and mindfully through their writing process in German and English, meeting goals from personal insight to well-being and professional growth.

37

School Choice

by Joanne Horn

A s I peered into the classroom from the oversized doorway, I saw a sunny room with the usual arrangement of rows of students at their desks, all facing the blackboard and teacher's desk. Behind them was a whole wall of open casement windows. The young, attractive teacher raised her hand to beckon me into the room. A cool breeze of relief washed over me as I stepped across the threshold. Introduced by Miss Fellows as "our new student" to the rest of her third-graders at Central Elementary, I felt welcome and hopeful for the first time since I had started elementary school.

Two years earlier, in first grade at St. Mary's Catholic School, I dreaded the arithmetic lesson. One student at a time, we were required to do the daily math problem on the blackboard in front of the whole class. As soon as my name was called and I slowly approached that endless expanse of blackboard, any recollection of how to add or subtract vanished from my mind. I would stand, staring blankly at the rows and columns of numbers, feeling the sweat slide down the stiff collar of my school uniform, waiting for Sister Mary Veronica's patience to wane. Inevitably I'd hear, "You may take your seat," and I'd be able to leave the frightening spotlight not having learned anything at all about arithmetic.

At St. Mary's, all the girls wore the same maroon and hunter-green plaid jumper and a white blouse with a Peter-Pan collar. It was strictly forbidden to wear any other clothing to school, even any other white blouse. Alas, from time to time at my house, when my mother would help my brother, Rich, and I get organized for school on Sunday evening, I'd realize I was in trouble.

"Mums," I'd whine, "I have to have the white blouse with the round collar. This isn't the right one."

"Oh, honey, it doesn't matter. This one is perfectly fine. It's pretty close to the uniform blouse. The others are in the wash. Tomorrow is washday. No one will even notice."

"No, Mums, I have to have the right blouse," I'd insist as I stamped my feet in frustration. "I can't go to school with the wrong one. Sister will yell at me!"

"Don't be ridiculous. You're telling me that they're going to have a problem if you show up with a different shirt one day of the week? That's absurd," she'd exclaim with her own bit of exasperation beginning to flair.

Seeing that I was on the verge of tears, Mums would put her arm around me and reassure me, "It's going to be OK, Joanne. I will talk to the nuns tomorrow when you go to school and explain the whole situation."

"OK, but promise you won't forget," I'd beg, only partially reassured. I knew Sister Mary Veronica would give me that disapproving stare no matter what Mums said. Those nuns, identical in their habit of chastity with their oversized rosaries tinkling and swinging like chains from their waists, worshiped conformity. There were no excuses. The wrong blouse was a sin.

The following year, at St. Stephen's Catholic School, I was assigned to a class in which second and third graders were combined together. Sister Mary Aloysius, somewhat stooped and bulging out of her starched white wimple and black habit, struggled to corral fifty energetic seven- and eight-year-olds through the lessons of each day.

I was naturally gregarious, and most subjects came easily to me, with the exception of arithmetic, for which I retained a fair amount of anxiety. I was always ready and willing to help my classmates who whispered,

"Joanne, what does she want us to do?" or "Do you understand where we are?" Most students, it seemed, were shy and not at all interested in risking the icy glare and stern countenance of Sister Mary Aloysius. Unfortunately for me, Sister's most important rule was "No Talking." Thus began my fairly regular attendance in after-school detention. The worst part about detention was that I would have to miss my bus, and my mother would have to rearrange her schedule to come pick me up an hour later.

One day, as I marched single file to detention, another nun whose name I didn't even know, leaned over and hissed, "You are a bold child." Although I had no idea what bold meant at the time, this outraged nun's tone indicated that it definitely wasn't good.

Toward the end of the school year, it was the ceramic planter incident that clarified for me—and, more importantly, for my parents—that St. Stephen's wasn't the best school for me. Each day, when the bell signaled the end of the school day, we were allowed to stand up next to our desks and put on our coats. This particular day, as I was getting into my spring jacket, suddenly the crash of china hitting the ground focused the attention of Sister Mary Aloysius on my row of desks next to the window. When she realized that it was her ceramic planter with its potted Philodendron that had been knocked onto the floor and crushed into smithereens, she began to scream. "Class, sit down! Who did that? No one is leaving this room until the student that did this admits it!"

As she was yelling, I realized that the planter had been sitting on the window ledge just opposite my desk and that when I put on my coat, without realizing it, the arm of my jacket must have brushed the planter off its small ledge. Terrified, I slowly raised my hand.

The next year, my parents removed me from the Catholic school system and enrolled me in the public school at Central Elementary. From that first moment at the threshold of my third-grade classroom, my educational experience completely turned around from one in which I was perceived as an unruly, bold troublemaker to one in which my curiosity, enthusiastic personality, and love of learning were allowed to grow and flourish.

My parents recognized that it was the school system and not me that needed to be adjusted. For that, I will always be grateful. As soon as I was introduced to an open learning environment, one that was capable of accommodating individual expression and not intent upon total discipline at all costs, I could find myself and be myself—and that has made all the difference in my life.

***

Joanne Horn has been a human relations specialist for three decades. From 1987 to 2007, she provided mediation, facilitation, and conflict management through her firm Conflict Resolution Service, Inc. In 2009, Joanne established Second Half Connections, helping students find renewed meaning and direction later in life. For her own "second half" work, Joanne earned her Guided Autobiography instructor certificate through the Birren Center and Geriatric Mental Health and Memoir Writing certificates from the University of Washington.

38

Ms. Patricia's Wild Ride

by Patricia Hamilton

M ost people have no trouble identifying their major life's crossroads. Not me. Instead of long, straight stretches interrupted by arrivals at major intersections where choices must be made—college graduation, marriage, children, career changes—my crazy life is more like "Mr. Toad's Wild Ride." This short story first appeared in 1908 in the popular children's book, *The Wind and the Willows*, by Kenneth Grahame—though many of us know it better as an attraction at Disneyland. Here's my version, starting with a movie treatment:

Ms. Toad's Wild Ride to Pacific Grove

Patricia Hamilton's classic Everywoman's Tale comes to life in this outrageous tragic-comedic saga filled with danger, high-spirited antics, and adventure! Bring the whole family along on Ms. Patricia's Wild Ride, a live-action faux-fantasy adapted from the pages of her classic *The California Woman* and commemorating the unforgettable encounters with Ancestors and Family, Friends and Teachers, Husbands, Children and Grandchildren, Bosses, Mentors, and Clients.

How It All Began

"The hour of birth has come!" said the Badger with great solemnity. "Whose hour?" asked the Rat, uneasily looking around. Mole busied himself with travel preparations. "Why, Ms. Toad's hour! The hour of

Toad! We'll teach her to be a sensible Toad, to drive her powerful Limousine of Life, set to begin in Surprise Valley this very day, March 30, 1946!"

They reached the Native Daughters of the Golden West Lane to Toad Hall in Cedarville, California, to find, as Badger had anticipated, a shiny newborn life, known hereafter as Ms. Patricia Ann Hamilton. She received her own unique genetic Nature from the twenty-three ancestral families that arrived in this country before 1776—a true Daughter of the American Revolution. Her Nurture would be by two well-meaning parents who really hadn't a clue. Ms. Patricia came, carried down the steps of the hospital, innocent and oblivious, sucking her thumb—and before Badger, Rat, or Mole could counsel either parent, she was whisked away in Dad's Hudson Hornet, off and away on the uncharted road of a life less traveled!

Trapped in the Ancestral Family Car

The Ancestral Family car proved powerful beyond belief! Father Farmer was at the wheel, Mother Gentry by his side, and seven assorted offspring hanging on for dear life. Father's predispositions sped them wildly along country roads, frantic years of residing briefly in small towns up and down the West Coast, seeing sights, briefly making then leaving all friends and extended families far behind. Careening, reeling with Mother's literary genes, they thrummed through libraries, where Ms. Patricia was flooded with a love for books, following her already insatiable curiosity and love of life.

With no real supervision, the car repeatedly spun out of control. Before the age of five, Ms. Patricia had: fallen out of the car on the way to Grandmother's house, lost her ear when Father ran over her with farm machinery, recovered from a concussion after doctors said she wouldn't, and she nearly drowned in a reservoir, only to be resuscitated by her older sister, Lorraine.

While narrowly avoiding preachers of hellfire and damnation at every holy-roller sanctum—to survive intact and hope someday to thrive—Ms. Patricia retreated into her own determined and imaginative inner world, supported with genetic resilience and flexibility and her predilection for happiness.

Taking the Wheel

Bailing out of the family conveyance at age eighteen, Ms. Patricia boarded a Greyhound bus from Oregon to California, right back where she had started. Now at the wheel of a new Toyota Celica and following in Father's vein, she flew at high speeds past bosses, burst through all glass ceilings, and rolled over every husband. During a powerful tsunami, as the vehicle began dangerously drifting sideways, she lost the grasp of her little daughter's hand. Life was going too fast and too furious when Ms. Patricia crashed full speed into the 1990s—alone.

Safe Harbor at Last!

Awakened by grace, she corrected with a sharp right turn and sped off in new and uncharted territory. Ms. Patricia headed for an ancestral safe harbor with her mother's twin, Aunt Charlotte, in Pacific Grove, California. Ms. Toad's Wild Ride came to an end in 1990, and at last the sensible time of her life began.

Ms. Patricia shed all transportation and took to walking and reflecting while on the Recreation Trail alongside Monterey Bay. Life experiences were examined, lessons were learned, college degrees earned, and visits were made to Ice Age ancestral sites in the United Kingdom, France, Spain, and Turkey. Transcendental meditation, mentors, and sea air restored her mind, body, and soul. She established her own book publishing company, where clients became lifelong friends. She welcomed her daughter, son-in-law, and two exceptional grandchildren to share in her good fortune. And she now follows the advice of her good friend Leonard Epstein to "Change your thinking, change your life. Give thanks and expect more!"

Epilogue

"Very well, then, Ms. Patricia," said Badger firmly, Rat and Mole looking on. "You've learned to be a sensible Toad, to Nurture your Nature and to thoughtfully maneuver your newest and most powerful Limousine of Life (aka Subaru Forester). We knew you would!"

***

Since 1983, Patricia Hamilton's company Park Place Publications has helped hundreds of authors achieve their dream of seeing their life story appear in print. In January 2022, she will complete her mission to produce ten books about her community—all with the goal of bringing people together through the power of story.

39

Finding My Way

by Ramona Charles

I occasionally heard my dad and his youngest brother plotting to send my older brother to college. Uncle Art would advance money to Larry. After graduation, Larry would help one or more of the younger brothers, and on down the line.

My sister and I were never part of the plan. Initially, I was content with my own plans to attend Saint Joseph Hospital School of Nursing.

In my early teens, the bus route took me from our South Louisville neighborhood to the transfer spot at the corner of Preston Highway and Eastern Parkway. As I stood waiting for the next bus, I was overshadowed by Our Mother of Sorrow Church covering most of the block on the south side of the parkway, and Saint Joseph Hospital dominating the entire block on the north side.

This was my known world.

Two weeks before my sixteenth birthday, our family of nine moved from our modern brick house in Louisville into a hundred-year-old farmhouse a couple of miles outside of Winchester. That was the year they closed the bedspring factory where my Dad had worked most of my life and relocated one hundred miles east from Louisville to Winchester, Kentucky, a small city of about 15,000 where labor costs were cheap. The consolidated county high school was miles away. There were no city buses. Saint Joseph Hospital School of Nursing was less accessible, and I was less content.

When I learned about Good Samaritan School of Nursing in
Lexington, I couldn't muster my enthusiasm. Other students in my school
would be going to the new nursing program at Eastern Kentucky
University. Being on a coed campus sounded more fun than being
cloistered in a female residence at a hospital.

I got a recruitment brochure about Eastern and started talking out loud
about college.

One day during the winter holidays, I was curled in a large chair in our
living room reading a novel when my dad came to the wide, arched
doorway across the room. He didn't come all the way in or sit down.

Dad shared that one of his bosses at the factory told him that I should
check into Berea College. The college had a work-study program, did not
charge tuition, and offered a nursing major. After dutifully sharing the
information, Dad called for my brother to help him bring in firewood and
left the room.

I remained restless until I got back to school.

Monday morning, I went to the school counselor's office and found a
brochure for Berea College. I carried the brochure home and spoke to no
one. The brochure described an undergraduate college with a little over
1,000 students. Admission required both academic standards and
financial need. No students were allowed cars on campus, and everyone
was assigned a job. The college was located another fifty miles down the
highway at the edge of the Appalachian Mountains.

I was back in the counselor's office, this time to ask if Berea was
something I could do. After all, I ranked seventh in a class of almost
three hundred.

He looked at my brochure and then at me. "Yes, Berea might be a
good place for you to find a husband."

I went still, stunned for a moment, then picked up my brochure and
left.

The next weekend, I sat at our kitchen table with the brochures for
Eastern and Berea laid out in front of me. Eastern was large and looked
busy. I could become an RN in just two years and begin earning money.

Berea looked serene, comfortable, an idyllic fairy tale of a college. Both schools were coed.

On a scratchpad, I lined out the money I would need to borrow to attend either college. The column for Eastern included room and board, books, and tuition right at $2,000 a year, and the Berea column included room and board and books at about $1,000 a year. Each option meant borrowing $4,000.

Four years of college for the price of two had to be the best deal.

In 1970 I became the first Registered Nurse at Clark County Hospital with a bachelor's degree.

And, by the way, the year I graduated, I married a wonderful man whom I had met at Berea College.

***

Ramona Charles became interested in memoir after retiring from a career in nursing administration. She is a widow, a mother, and a grandmother. She trained in Guided Autobiography in 2016 and offers classes at continuing education venues. Originally from Kentucky, she now lives in Cleveland, Ohio.

40

Generally Healthy

by Karen Bender

"Are you generally healthy?"

The question stopped me cold as I filled out the new patient form.

Previous answers had come to me effortlessly. Name, address, insurance information. Emergency contact. Did I have, or had I ever had, cancer, diabetes, stroke? No, no, no.

And then the seemingly philosophical: "Are you generally healthy?"

I had no idea how to respond. I was only visiting the dermatologist that day because the rigorous swimming routine I had adopted was affecting my skin. My arms and legs had become red and itchy from the chlorine, and I needed some sort of cream, I assumed, to soothe them. The swimming ritual alone should qualify me as generally healthy, I reasoned. I could almost hear my inner voice imploring the pen to move.

But then there was the MS. Multiple sclerosis had been my wearisome sidekick for over a decade at that point.

When I think back, I'm genuinely not certain which box I checked. The truth is I'd already learned that sharing my diagnosis with some doctors muddied waters that needn't be muddied. How many rabbit holes had I gone down, insisting the MS was not to blame for my ear pain or backache or twisted ankle? It's very possible that I deemed myself "generally healthy" solely to ensure a quick doctor's visit, one that didn't necessitate a referral to a specialist.

But the question lingered for me long after I left the dermatologist's doors, and I found myself weighing the yes and no responses for months. I have a normal life expectancy, I reasoned. I'm not contagious. Nobody would know I have MS unless I told them. I work and parent and socialize and travel. Overall, I feel good and happy and, yes, "generally healthy."

Except, of course, I had bad days too. Days when I felt like my legs had been crushed by a truck and my eyes had been set on fire. Always, I lived with the certainty that even a light workout would raise my body temperature enough to bring on pins and needles or numbness. My fingertips felt no sensation at all. I needed more sleep than my elementary-aged son, and I took more medications than my septuagenarian father.

Usually, I handled my symptoms well. They simply were a part of who I was. Writer, mother, wife, MS patient, daughter, friend. But I did have my moments. Moments when the chronic reality of this chronic disease broke through, and my easy acceptance fell away. Moments when I crumbled under the weight of it all.

***

Last summer, we received a postcard from the National MS Society. The DC chapter was inviting local kids who have a parent with MS to meet the Washington Nationals superstar, Ryan Zimmerman. Zimmerman, I learned, had adopted MS as his charity of choice, as his own mother has the disease.

My son literally jumped out of his chair when he saw the postcard lying on the kitchen table. "I can meet Ryan Zimmerman?"

Evan lives for baseball. It's his greatest passion, his hoped-for career, and the chance to meet this hometown hero made his eyes pop.

Without even thinking, I tried to talk him down. "But you're a Mets fan," I reminded him. "And it's just for kids. Daddy and I aren't invited."

"That's ok," he countered. "Ryan Zimmerman!"

I paused, noting a tinge of discomfort creeping in.

"I'll talk to Daddy," I recovered. Anything to put him off.

Later that evening, when I had a moment to myself, I revisited the conversation. At first, I chalked up my hesitancy to principle. While my son was certainly eligible to attend, I felt that these kinds of events should be reserved for kids who are genuinely impacted by their parent's illness. For kids who have to make the family's dinner every night because Mom or Dad can't handle the preparation. For kids who can't join Little League because nobody can drive them there. Evan had none of these limitations, and I didn't know if he should participate in light of that. Declining a spot would be the noble decision.

But I also sensed there was more to this. Something less abstract. And eventually, after digging just a bit deeper, it came to me.

At its core, this invitation re-opened the very personal question I had finally pushed away: Am I generally healthy? Because if I was, how could I let my son attend this event? (He didn't belong there!) And if I wasn't, well, what did that mean for me?

In the end, for reasons we couldn't fully articulate, my husband and I decided to let Evan go. We fleetingly wondered if it might be good for him to see that there are other kids who have a parent with the same mysterious two-lettered illness that I have. And sure, Evan saw me tired and overheated sometimes. He helped me with buttons and zippers when my fingers proved futile. Maybe he did feel some impact of the disease.

Truthfully, though, it was Evan's own pleading that forced our verdict. He was invited, he wanted to go. We said okay.

Maybe it wasn't a reflection of me after all.

***

Last October, a little girl in our community died from a brain tumor. Gabriella was bright and beautiful and vibrant. She was awe-inspiring, and she spent the last eleven months of her life advocating for pediatric cancer awareness and funding. Gabriella captured the love of thousands, if not millions, thanks to the Internet, and we were all devastated when she passed.

I never met Gabriella, but her death impacted me profoundly. Why her? Why a young child with a beautiful heart, astounding mind, and endless possibilities ahead?

She was ten years old when she died.

I cried for a mother unknown to me.

The cruelty of it was hard for me to reconcile.

***

And so it was that an answer finally arrived.

With both acceptance and grace.

Am I generally healthy?

Probably not.

But I'm healthy enough.

***

Karen Bender helps ordinary people write their extraordinary stories. She works with clients one-on-one, creating full-length books that share full-length journeys, and in groups where workshop participants explore some of life's most meaningful themes. Karen is a big believer in the healing power of autobiographical writing.

41

The Fortunate Volunteer

by Frances Corry

The greatest crossroads in my life happened when I was seventeen years old. I signed up for a final backpacking trip in the Canadian Rocky Mountains through Camp Manito-wish, a YMCA summer camp in northern Wisconsin I had attended every summer since I was fourteen. This camp was my haven.

Rather than spend my summers working on a swimsuit tan, or my soccer skills, or moving up in popularity with middle school and high school friends, I saved up all my babysitting money and went to camp. There, I learned how to steer and portage a canoe, carry a heavy pack up a mountain, and work on being a leader in the out of doors. My core confidence came from putting every ounce of strength and faith I had into climbing a mountain. I reached outside of my comfort zone, doing things I did not think I was capable of doing. I accessed my inner resources, the strength of my soul, which helped me realize that there was much more to me than meets the eye.

After four summers in a row, the final outpost trip the camp offered was thirty-six days backpacking, rock climbing, and mountaineering in the Canadian Rockies. My friends, whom I had grown so fond of from summers together in the wilderness, had parents who were willing and able to fund their camp experiences.

But my father told me, "If you want to go to camp this summer, you will have to come up with the money on your own."

There was no way I could earn $2,700 on the weekends babysitting! So I called the camp director and told him my predicament. He came back with an offer, a "campership." Sort of like a scholarship, but I would earn the funds. Camp would fund $2,000 of the cost, and I would earn it by volunteering in my community. My volunteer hours would go toward the scholarship. Little did I know that the "random" place I decided to volunteer would turn into my life's work!

I decided to volunteer at Oakwood Village Nursing home. I visited two lonely residents a couple of times a week, providing them comfort and companionship. What I found was a true, lasting, intergenerational bond. The summer of backpacking came and went. It was a trip that I will remember for the rest of my life. But what was more impactful? I kept the volunteer job long after I had completed my campership obligation.

I stayed close to those companions until they died. Then I began working in the memory care unit at Oakwood to pay for college, realizing that I had a calling to work with elders and their stories.

Oakwood funded me to do a project that I came up with called "Wisdom of the Elders," where I interviewed a hundred elders in the nursing home, forty with dementia and sixty without. I asked them what they had learned in their lives that they wanted to pass down to future generations. This small book that we self-published was a treasure to the residents' families and even used in empathy training for the new staff.

I now have a Bachelor's in creative writing and a Master's in social work with a focus on geriatrics. I tailored my Master's degree at the University of Chicago to older adults and, more specifically, hospice care. While working in hospice after graduation, I came across the Birren Center for Guided Autobiography (GAB). As a writer, the training was fulfilling for me, and I learned so much about myself! My employer thought the process of GAB was so valuable that they allowed it to be part of my job description to go into the community and start GAB groups.

Of all the senior homes where I taught Guided Autobiography, there was one senior home that stuck out the most. Before I introduced GAB, the activity instructor told me that the seniors did not mingle and spent a lot of time isolated. After three GAB groups, the whole tone changed. Seniors were getting together for "fireside chats." After I stopped doing GAB groups there, my last group continued to meet and came up with their own writing prompts!

One thing I love to foster in people is good listening skills. As the quote goes, "The biggest communication problem is that we do not listen to understand. We listen to reply." I teach my participants about active listening. When one member is reading, I instruct the listeners to write down whatever they hear that strikes their curiosity and empathy. Never to edit, but to comment in a way that increases connection. These members get so close through truly listening and witnessing each other.

One witness I will always remember was a man named Jim. A few months after our GAB class was completed, one of the men in the circle let me know Jim had died. I called Jim's daughter to express my condolences. When I introduced myself as Jim's guided autobiography instructor, she said, "You. You're the one who taught my dad how to tell his story. Our whole lives, he did not tell us anything about himself until he took your course. He began telling his story. His stories healed him. Even on his deathbed, he was still telling us his story."

This may be the best and most meaningful affirmation I have ever, and could ever, hope to receive. The wonderful thing about GAB is that it has combined the things I love – creative expression through writing, active listening, formation of community and fellowship, self-exploration, finding a new calling, and finding meaning in life. Finding the Birren Center was like stumbling upon a pot of gold.

Through the camp director's generous idea for me to give back to my community so I could go to camp, I discovered my vocation and my calling, my life's work. For that, I am forever grateful.

***

Frances Corry is an advanced practice social worker with a love for creative expression. With a Master's degree in social work from the

University of Chicago and a Bachelor's from the University of Wisconsin Madison in English/Creative Writing, she combines these skills to foster a safe and healing space for people to write their life stories.

42

Kidnapping Mother

by Val Perry

"**N**o, it's too late for me. I am not moving to America now," said our mother, jutting her chin defiantly. My eldest brother, Dave, and I recognized that look on her face from years gone by and knew her mind was set. Discussion over.

The year was 2007, and I had just offered to be her caregiver if she would let me move her from England to my home in Florida. I was the obvious choice since Dave was still working in Australia.

Each yearly visit after that, I became increasingly concerned about my mother's health. She was a fiercely independent woman but had become isolated, especially after she stopped driving. From her neat apartment on the edge of town, she took a taxi each afternoon to the center of Epping to shop. I noticed her walk was now a shuffle instead of the confident stride I remembered. Most alarming was her confusion and loss of memory. In 2014 I cajoled her into taking a medical test, and she received the diagnosis I had feared, Alzheimer's disease.

Five months later, in November, I became concerned enough to make a return visit to the UK. Within a few days of my arrival, I received a frantic call at the hotel from Mother's building manager saying I needed to come immediately. By the time I arrived, there was an ambulance blocking the entranceway, and two men were wheeling my mother out on a gurney. She had dislocated her left shoulder in a fall.

Mum stayed in hospital for two weeks, and I became curious how she was coping with the prohibition on smoking. She had a two-pack-a-day habit. During one hospital visit, she smacked her mouth and said, "I feel like there is something I want in my mouth." I quickly fished out a packet of biscuits from my purse and said, "Here, you're probably hungry." When I left, she was still contently munching.

Mum was well-liked. I often found one of her old caregivers, on their own time, happily sitting next to her hospital bed. One day, my taxi driver identified himself as Joe, the man who regularly drove my mother into town. His round, jovial face became serious when he said, "Maybe it's because I'm Italian and, y'know, we love our mothers, but I think your momma needs more care."

A turning point came when Mum's hospital doctor said she would not release my mother unless I guaranteed her twenty-four-hour care. To afford this, we would have to sell Mum's apartment, which would take some time. That evening I called my husband in Florida and Dave in Australia. My husband simply said, "Bring her back with you," and Dave agreed. In less than one hour, a life-changing decision was made. This could be done because both Dave and I were Mother's power of attorney for her health and finances.

Over the next few days, I purchased Mum a ticket to Tampa and packed her summer clothes in an old suitcase from her closet. I located her current passport and miraculously found travel insurance for an eighty-seven-year-old woman. I was given a three-month supply of her medications and purchased a lightweight, collapsible wheelchair I hoped I could lift and steer when the time came.

With Mum's discharge papers in hand, I arranged to leave the hospital at 6:30 a.m. on November 27. Joe drove me to the hospital entrance and later to the airport. The sky that morning was pitch black and the air chilly. Of course, it was raining. I saw the nurse standing behind my mother's wheelchair in the lighted foyer, and I wondered, *Can I do this?*

"When are we going to be home?" Mum asked repeatedly as she peered out the taxi window into the passing dark landscape. Did she guess what was happening? If she did, she never let on.

An hour later, we arrived at Gatwick airport. Joe stood on the sidewalk next to me and Mum in her new wheelchair. I paid him and he smiled, looking down into my eyes for a long while. Then he bent down to Mum and said, "I'm glad you're feeling better, Mrs. Young. I know your daughter will take good care of you."

For ninety minutes, I pushed Mum around the British Airways departure lounge amid hundreds of people busily eating and shopping. I had quite a workout keeping away from the large displays of cigarettes in the duty-free shops. As a safeguard, I purchased Mum a box of English biscuits and, when asked, told her we were at a shopping mall.

Since we had the wheelchair, Mum and I were amongst the first to board the plane and were safely installed side by side in Business Class by the time the other passengers began pushing their way down the aisles.

"Where are we now? Mum asked.

"At the movies," I replied without hesitation. *Oh my goodness, I'm getting way too good at this,* I thought.

We watched a musical, and when the food trays came around, she enjoyed the lemon chicken and wanted second helpings of the chocolate mousse. I reluctantly gave her mine, although I really could have used some chocolate right then.

"Val, I need the toilet," Mum said.

I had dreaded this moment. The steward advised me to use the back bathrooms as they were slightly larger. She then unfolded a small version of a wheelchair with no arms, and we struggled to lift Mum onto the device. Three other stewards appeared; I got the feeling this chair was not used very often. Soon all six of us were shimmying down towards the back of the aircraft at some speed, causing surprised passengers to dive back into their seats as we approached. I led the procession and helped pull the chair back into the toilet stall behind me. Just as the door closed, I realized that it was Mum who needed to be by the toilet bowl, not me. Seconds later, to the surprise of the waiting stewards, Mum and I came barreling out and switched places. I noticed Mum was smiling. She always enjoyed a bit of excitement.

About six hours into our twelve-hour journey, I mentioned we were on an airplane. It just came out.

"WHAT ARE WE DOING ON AN AIRPLANE?" Mother shouted, her eyes wide.

Over and over, I explained where we were going, the hospital's demand for her care, and yes, I had packed her raincoat, and on and on. When I hesitated, she would begin shouting to everyone around us.

At last, the nightmare flight came to an end. I have never been so thankful to see my husband and daughter waiting for us at the gate.

My mother lived happily in Florida for twenty-eight months before she died. During that time, she received her green card, the Affordable Care Act passed, and we met some of the kindest, most generous people in our community. I learned that caring for a parent can be exhausting but a privilege.

Mum never smoked again after her shoulder injury; however, on our drive home from the airport that first night, we stopped at McDonald's to pick up a quick dinner. As we came up to the drive-thru window, my mother, sitting in the front seat, suddenly leaned forward and shouted to the server, "Do you have a packet of Salem and a lighter?"

***

Val Perry was born and grew up in London. As an adult, she lived in both the US and England before retiring to Valrico, Florida, with her husband, daughter, and tuxedo cat, Gracie. Val has led a life writing program and taught Guided Autobiography classes at her local library for fifteen years.

PART 3 | Change

If we don't change, we don't grow.
If we don't grow, we aren't really living.

— Gail Sheehy

43

The Voice Lesson

by Arlene Higgs

I t's a beautiful July day in Calgary, Alberta, barely a month since I graduated from Crescent Heights High School. I hear footsteps on the front porch, and then the doorbell rings. Our guest has arrived.

Before I go to the door, I check that my belt is still done up. I'm wearing the summer dress that I just finished sewing, and the clasp hasn't turned out to be very secure. Oh well, too late to change.

Mr. Riggs is younger than I expected, perhaps in his mid-thirties, handsome in the meaty way of current male movie stars: James Garner, say, or Bob Goulet. I'm only sixteen, but he tells me to call him Seth. He smiles, talks brightly, and radiates an unusual assurance and intensity.

I'm a bit embarrassed for him, then decide that it's probably just that he's from the United States. The grownup Canadian men I know – my teachers, my Dad's friends, my uncles, my choir director, the minister who leads my church youth group – are, without exception, reserved and quiet.

Maybe what I've heard Dad say is true: Americans are all a little bit full of themselves.

Seth is from New York. He's a singer and actor in musical theatre who has just flown in to perform at the 1964 Calgary Stampede. He'll star in the nightly Grandstand Show. He is also a vocal coach, and it has been arranged that today he will give me a voice lesson here in my home.

Mom and Dad come to the door, greeting him with the hearty good cheer they reserve for company. Dad shakes Seth's hand, man-to-man. "Nice to meet you. Come in, come in."

Dad has come home from the office for lunch, and he's wearing his cowboy shirt with a bolo tie. Since this is Stampede Week, he pretty much has to; it's company policy. For the outdoor events, he sports a beautiful white felt cowboy hat.

Mom is looking spiffy in her full skirt, white ankle socks, and sandals. She has fluffed out her perm and applied fresh lipstick, I'm guessing Revlon Hot Coral, her favourite colour. She leads us into the dining room, where she's laid out the good china and table linen. I stare at the setup for a moment and am about to tease her about it. *Why all this? It's not as if today's a holiday.* But I think better of it. She tells us where to sit, then passes around the lunch she's prepared: a platter with thick slices of cold ham, crystal dishes filled with homemade sweet pickles, and a bowl of potato salad with chopped celery and Miracle Whip. The grownups sip black coffee. I have a glass of milk.

They make small talk. *How was your flight... What do you think of Calgary? Beautiful city... Lovely house... Such a nice meal.* Mom serves the apple pie that she baked this morning. I watch the three of them do their polite social thing. Mom tells Seth that she's never been to New York and asks him too many questions, "What is it like to live in such a huge, busy city? Tell us about the Broadway shows you've been in."

I frown and look down at my hands. *Thanks, Mom, for confirming that we're a bunch of small-town hicks.*

Then, because I'm the sole reason for this stilted little gathering, the spotlight is on me. My singing, my plans to study in New York, my dreams for a future in music. Seth asks me questions, and I answer, aware that the three of them are watching me. Usually, I don't mind being centre stage, but today I'm uncomfortable, and for some reason, think of a livestock auction ring, with me being led round and round.

At last, Seth and I go into the living room where the piano is. Mom and Dad excuse themselves, but I know darn well they'll be listening from the other room. This realization settles on me like a heavy blanket. Dad doesn't usually stay home for such a long lunch break. *Why doesn't he just get back to the office?* I can feel my jaw clenching with the need to be away from them.

We start the lesson with a few arpeggios. *Relax your jaw ... breathe from your diaphragm ... keep the air flowing.* So far, no different from my usual lessons with Mr. Erickson, who is my Calgary voice teacher, a plump old man whom I would never dare to call by his first name. Mr. Erickson gives lessons at his studio, a nice private place where nobody can hear us making the peculiar noises distinctive to a serious vocal workout.

Here at home, I feel exposed. "Well, at least the neighbours will have a good laugh," I joke. This living room, indeed this whole house, suddenly seems cramped. It's too small for Seth's bold gestures and big baritone voice.

But we carry on. To demonstrate the proper in-and-out breathing movements, he takes my hands and holds them against each side of his muscular torso. I know it's just a teaching technique, probably the way they all do it in New York, but his face is too close to mine, and I feel myself flush. I pull my hands back, but not too fast, so I won't seem rude or naive.

Then he introduces something new to me: the concept of the middle passage, or *passaggio.* This, he announces, is the unstable transition between a vocalist's low and high ranges, and it's something all singers have to work very hard to master. He demonstrates by singing a long scale in full voice, and I listen hard as his notes flow evenly along like a broad river of sound. He gives me the note for my scale and I try.

My voice starts off smooth at the bottom and ends up smooth at the top, but in between, it wavers and stumbles. *Open up your throat. Relax your tongue.* I try again and fail again. Although he's a good teacher and the two of us keep at it for a while, I can't get the hang of it. Finally, to my relief, the lesson comes to an end. Mom and Dad appear, and we get through the polite thank-yous and good-byes.

That night, while Seth belted out his big numbers to the Stampede crowds, my high school ensemble sang backup for him. A souvenir album of the show was produced and named for the show, *Shoot for the Stars*. Seth's aim was high and true. Eventually, he became a vocal coach to such legends as Barbra Streisand, Stevie Wonder, Michael Jackson, and Madonna.

I moved to New York City for university and never lived on the prairies again. That summer of 1964 was the last time I saw Seth. It was the summer that I stopped wanting to be Mom and Dad's prize filly, but didn't know how to be anything else. The year I thought I was too big for Calgary.

What I didn't know – couldn't have known – was how vast New York was going to be. How much I was going to have to learn. How very hard it was going to be to cross the *passaggio*.

***

Arlene Higgs started writing her memoirs at the age of seventy-two during the coronavirus shutdown, inspired by a Guided Autobiography course led by Wendy Bancroft. She is the mother of two daughters and lives in Vancouver, British Columbia, with her husband.

44

The Hot Peppers of Hunan

by Philip Holden

In 1986, when I was twenty-four, I took the longest flight I'd ever taken. I started in Gainesville, Florida, with a brand-new master's degree and two bulging, battered black suitcases that barely snuck under my weight allowance. I first flew to Atlanta in a small plane, then transferred to a transcontinental flight headed for San Francisco. That flight was delayed, and I had to run through the San Francisco airport to make my connecting flight to Tokyo. Because this leg had been overbooked, I was rewarded with my first ever experience of sitting in Business Class with a seat the size of an armchair.

I sat next to a Japanese father and son feasting on sushi and other unexpected delights. The son promptly threw up. The father, mortified, apologized profusely. In Tokyo, we changed planes again, and I flew on to Beijing. We arrived late at night, and as we circled, our pilot told us that the runway lights had been switched off for the night and he had asked that they be switched back on. At the airport, I experienced another first: a young man, holding a board with my name written on it, was waiting for me.

Two days later, my new companion and I flew south in a propeller-driven plane that moved with infinite slowness. My companion had never travelled by air before, and I offered him a window seat. We passed over the Yellow River and then the Yangtze. It was another hot evening when we descended again, on a thin runway flanked by ancient fighter planes.

For the final part of my journey, we went by car, a magnificent black Shanghai Saloon that reminded me of the old Mercedes Benz that my father drove when I was a child. My companion and I bounced around on the backseat over uneven roads, our horn sounding occasionally as we passed through a sea of bicycles. We crossed a bridge, turned right, then left, and under a concrete arch with cursive characters that I would only later come to read: 湖南师范大学, "Hunan Normal University." The car continued uphill on a concrete path that seemed to grow ever narrower until we got to the very highest building on campus, just underneath the water tower surrounded by pine trees.

More characters I could not yet read: 专家楼 Zhuānjiā lóu, "Expert Building." This was where I would live, where I would prepare my lectures and seminars as a Foreign Expert, teaching graduate students English and American Literature. It was also a new beginning in my life. China up till now had been peripheral to me. Various forms of Chineseness would be a central part of the rest of my life, through histories, literature, and struggles to learn the language, and in most of my close friendships, including that with my life partner.

The China I came to was still emerging from the Cultural Revolution, only seven years after Deng Xiaoping's reforms began. On the street, most people still wore the blue or green Zhōngshānzhuāng, a Chinese tunic suit or jacket, although my students were experimenting with tweed jackets, skirts, makeup, and leather shoes.

As a foreign teacher, I was immensely privileged, but I still lost weight in the winter when fresh vegetables and food were in short supply. In the student canteen, all the dishes were spiced with the hot red chilies central to Hunanese cuisine and to Hunanese identity. The illuminated red flame on the tower of the city's train station, my students whispered, was, in fact, a giant chili. Didn't I know that all the great Chinese revolutionaries, from Mao Zedong to Deng Xiaoping, were from Hunan on Sichuan, their political passions inflamed by the hot peppers they ate?

In the evening, I would accompany them to a street-side stall just outside the university gate, perch on rough wooden benches, and eat chou dofu, "stinky tofu," black and rancid smelling, washed down with vinegar, garlic, and those inevitable chilies. Years later, in Taiwan, in Singapore, and San Francisco, I'd see the characters in a shop window or, more often, smell its distinctive odor. I'd hunt it down and eat a sanitized version of the original, golden instead of black, with a taste that still tapped into those memories.

I realise now that what most appealed to my students about my teaching was not my knowledge but an absence of it. I was like a child, full of hope, enthusiastic in my ignorance, unmarked by the burden of a history they had suffered through.

History was surely on my side. In 1987, Taiwan ended its ban on travel to Mainland China, and brothers and sisters of senior academics began arriving back in Changsha: families that had been separated for forty years were reunited. I watched and listened. In lessons I took from a private tutor in the Zhuānjiā lóu, I began my lifelong struggle with the Chinese language.

The world and I were at a crossroads, still more than two years before the June Fourth event in Tiananmen Square. I returned to my homeland physically but found that I was unable to feel at ease and soon departed. I travelled, I made new residences, but I would never quite be at home again. The world itself, at the end of the Cold War, seemed to come to a crossroads and take a wrong turn. Over the last twenty years, in particular, I feel we have chosen the wrong path. As if we were lost in the countryside, where the way is narrow and becomes rutted and uneven, but there is no longer space to turn around.

In my own memories, at least, I linger at the crossroads of possibility in Hunan in 1986 and wonder about the path I took, and the one the world chose not to take.

***

Philip Holden has spent his life on three continents. After a long academic career in Singapore, he now lives in Vancouver, Canada, where he is training as a counselor and a Guided Autobiography instructor.

45

The Bus

by Sandi Bojm

W e arrived at the parking lot of a strip mall in Pemberton. The sun was just beginning to rise. Diffused rays of light magnified the mist in the air on this cool August morning. I caught my reflection in the large window of the paint store. I looked haggard, in need of a hair wash and a good rest. Sleep had come in fits and starts, and the fleece jacket I had thrown on at the last minute was showing wear, with a small tear along the sleeve. I tucked my fist into the sleeve to make it slack. Maybe no one would notice. I made a mental note to take better care of myself. Maybe I would in the next three weeks.

Janna half-disappeared into the trunk, hauling out her gear. The hiking boots, tied together by the laces and attached to a side loop on her pack, swayed like a pendulum as she hoisted the pack onto her back. The sleeping bag and tarp were perched on top, cinched in two places by elastic straps. At five-foot-two, she seemed dwarfed by the whole contraption.

I thought I saw her wince, regain her balance, and then reach up to close the hatch. Wordlessly, she turned and headed across the lot. I followed, vaguely aware of the tight feeling in my throat.

Janna was fourteen. Her height had always been a sore point for her. Her younger brother had inherited the tall gene from my husband's side. Janna, on the other hand, took after my grandmother, a wisp of a thing, despite her personal strength. Janna was a trouper who never shied from challenges. We admired her ability to pick herself up after disappointments and keep going. She demonstrated great endurance and perseverance for her young age. I'm not sure she knew then how much we valued that in her.

As I watched her ahead of me in the lot, I remembered the obstacles we had both faced over the last year. The high school social scene was precarious. The values and interests of many same-aged kids didn't jive with her own. She was having trouble in math. As her mom, I felt her angst and moved in closer, trying to problem-solve. We did an extra hour of math tutoring every day. As I pursued, she backed away. I felt the rift, but like many parents, I wanted to fix things because I cared. Letting go and giving space was not so easy. In the spring, she announced her decision to do a vision quest, a three-week trek among the northern mountains and glaciers. I took a deep breath and agreed.

I caught sight of her short turquoise hair. She had recently cut and dyed it. Was it an act of defiance or a declaration of independence? Her hair had always been long and shiny with a soft wave through it. The thickness of it was both a gift and liability, a challenge to dry and a bit wild in humid weather, but it always drew compliments. I was shocked when she came home one evening, sporting a new look. "Hi, Dear, how was your day? And by the way, what have you done to your hair? No, I don't hate it, just surprised, is all."

It was the same story when, a month or so before that, she sported an unexpected nose ring. Thankfully it morphed into a tiny delicate gem tucked into the crease at the side of her nose. I came to like it, the way it glinted in the light.

There was a small group of kids milling about the yellow school bus. Packs were pulled off shoulders and heaved into the underbelly of the vehicle. Above the windows, it read *Pemberton S. D. 49*. I was strangely reassured by the familiarity of it. Parents and kids were engaged in good-byes. When I got closer, I heard pieces of conversation.

"Don't forget your meds."

"Stay safe."

"Enjoy."

Sparse words in quiet tones that matched the stillness of the early morning hour.

I watched the other parents with interest. Were they like Michael and me? Would they miss their kids as much? Or were they secretly relieved that there would be a bit of respite for a few weeks? Did they have the same uneasy feeling signing the waiver that spoke of potential accidents, injuries, bears, cougars, and even the remote possibility of death?

I wondered about the kids who seemed typical enough, sporting baseball caps, hoodies, and full of youthful curiosity. Normal hair colour. I zipped up my fleece as the wind picked up a bit.

A fellow with a clipboard approached the two of us. "You must be Janna. And you must be Janna's mom."

He looked about thirty, with blonde hair and a beard. He was tanned and rugged and immeasurably fit. His zipped jersey hugged the muscles of his forearms. I saw my fingers engulfed in the enormity of his handshake.

"I'm Conan," he said.

"Oh, like Conan O'Brien, the talk show host." It was my attempt at being sociable.

"Heh, yeah, well, more like Conan the Barbarian, I'd say." He laughed. I obliged him with a smile, but I knew it was forced. "Janna, just tuck your stuff in there and hop on. We'll be off soon." He didn't seem to notice her turquoise hair.

As Janna moved away, Conan put his big hand on my shoulder. "Don't worry, Mrs. Allen. She'll be fine. Anyway, gotta run." And with that, Conan jogged toward the bus driver. Most of the kids were already in their seats, while parents made their way back to their vehicles.

"Bye, Mom." A quick hug, and Janna was off. It was too abrupt.

It had taken more than a month to prep for this trip. I had researched and created an equipment list and carried it with me everywhere, perusing it in coffee shops and at night before bed. I read and reread it, crossing items off as I purchased them. Sometimes Janna came with me, but most of the time, I negotiated the stores on my own while she was in school. I was more comfortable without her looming impatience and embarrassment.

I had learned the benefits of certain fabrics in the wind, which ones stood the rigors of cold and wet, the strength of Gore-Tex, and different waterproofing products that would seal hiking boots. I could identify hiking boots that promised good traction and ankle support. I learned all about sleeping bags. Did we want down or synthetic, mummy-style or one with some wiggle room? I became a fount of knowledge about UV rays, blister protection, moisture-wicking, and hydration. I bought bear spray, bug spray, and a Swiss Army knife. I reached into my purse and fingered the tattered and well-worn list, still in the side pocket where I kept it.

The bus motor started up, and the broad tires began to lumber along the pavement. I watched it move to the far corner of the parking lot and down the driveway. I caught sight of a shock of turquoise through one of the windows. Janna seemed to be leaning against the glass. I thought I saw a faint wave of her hand, a sort of half-wave, noncommittal. The bus rolled into the distance, and then it turned north onto Highway 99.

A new journey had begun for both of us.

***

Sandi Bojm is a speech-language pathologist whose interest in her clients' stories and life contexts led her to become a counselling therapist. After taking several Guided Autobiography classes for her own enjoyment, she went on to become a GAB instructor in 2019. She recently compiled a book of her personal stories to share with her children and grandchildren.

46

Changing Course

by Christina Lyons

I gently knocked on the door to Granny's apartment, then entered. Peering into her bedroom, I saw the ninety-nine-year-old's gray hair splayed across the pillow, her thin form motionless under the blankets in the hot room. I took a deep breath and approached her bed. I was terrified, but I silently reminded myself that this was the new career I had chosen. I could do this.

My mind flashed back to the heartache and panic I felt several years earlier as I stood in the middle of the newsroom at my former job as an editor in Washington, DC. It was a Thursday in late September, 2009. Hours earlier, I had watched my co-editor, close colleagues, and friends clear out their desks and depart the building. The new management, under the guidance of the company's new owner, had given over forty editorial employees less than an hour to pack up and leave. My co-editor scrambled to box up his things, then quickly reminded me he had just filed a story that I needed to edit. I assured him I would.

Standing there, I wondered about this full-time journalism career I had worked so hard to pursue. I had known at a young age that all I wanted to do was write. In high school, while writing for the school newspaper, I decided a journalism career would be my future. It wasn't until I was in college at University of the Pacific in central California that I developed an interest in politics and history. As news editor of the college paper, I wrote about anything I fancied – from the board of regents' tuition increases to UOP Law Professor Anthony Kennedy's nomination to the Supreme Court. During my senior year, the newspaper advisor (newly arrived from President Reagan's White House press office) encouraged me to go east and look for a job.

For a few years, I worked on small newspapers in Maryland, learning the basics of local and state politics. From there, I went to Washington, DC, reporting on Capitol Hill while obtaining my Master's degree in political science. I eventually landed a short-term gig working on a documentary on Congress and the Media for Congressional Quarterly, a well-respected news company. The project led to a full-time, salaried editing job there.

My supervisors eventually allowed me to cut back my work hours to accommodate the needs of my young family. In 2007, I returned full-time to manage and co-edit a book of profiles of every member of Congress. The company's sale was announced just as the book came out. I had barely processed the news when I received a call from my father letting me know his wife had passed away. I jumped on a plane to Idaho to be with my father and help him plan a memorial.

My sister was already at my father's house in Idaho when I arrived. In her rush to remove any signs of our stepmother from their home, she had left piles of photographs spread on the floor in every room. My sister said she was trying to collect our stepmother's old family photographs to send to our stepbrothers. I settled in to help. As I peered into cabinets and drawers throughout the house, searching for more, I stumbled upon my father's military album and a very old family photo album. Nothing was labeled.

With gentle prodding, my father agreed to look through the albums with me. We spent the next two afternoons and evenings going through the photos. I peppered him with questions and kept detailed notes. He allowed me to remove the photos from the albums so I could match them with my notes and later scan and preserve them. The discussion elicited not just names of ancestors but many vivid stories I had never heard before.

After about five days with my father, I returned to home and work –
just in time for a send-off for my company's top editors who had been
laid off as part of the buyout.

The next night, a 3:00 a.m. phone call from my brother awakened my
husband and me. Dad had died in a car accident. I cried for hours,
shivering with cold from the shock as my husband held me. My two
young children, awakened by my loud sobs, huddled close.

I returned to Idaho with my family for a few days to make
arrangements with a funeral home and manage my father's affairs. When
I returned, I struggled to put my mind back into work during the day,
dashing home in the evenings to work on a video presentation of my
father's life to share at his memorial service set for October. The editorial
staff layoffs occurred weeks before that memorial service, leaving me in
a sea of empty desks. The path I was on was no longer clear.

I went to the executive editor and, failing to choke back tears, told
him, "I'm sorry, I can't stay here." He begged me to reconsider and, over
the next hour, tried to explain all of his decisions. "Please, stay a few
months and see how you feel." I agreed.

I spent the next few months agonizing, *Do I stay or do I go? Can I do
something more fulfilling with my talents, find some way to help people?*
I deeply wanted to do something with my writing, something important.

After three months of anguish, I made my choice. I would leave and
find a new path.

I took on some freelance writing while delving into my family history.
One day, my former co-editor pointed me to an association of personal
historians. I explored this new world, talking with members of the group
and attending conferences. After taking a certification course in life
reminiscence, I believed more strongly that this is why I had left
journalism. Here is where I might make a difference.

Arline – or "Granny," as everyone called her – was one of my early
interviewees. I had spent more than a year with her, listening for hours
each week as she described growing up on a farm in Ohio, attending
nursing school in Chicago, dating, becoming an Army nurse, and more.

As her health declined, I drafted a manuscript and placed it in a three-ring binder at her bedside. One holiday season, the end seemed near. Friends and relatives came to visit, one by one. She asked each of them to read a chapter of her story. Everyone obliged.

As I walked into her bedroom, two days before Christmas, I gently called, "Granny?" She opened her eyes, turned her head, and smiled. I breathed a quiet sigh of relief. She pushed herself up slightly and asked me how I was. Then she asked me to read a couple of chapters of her story. I watched as her mind wandered back to the 1920s and 1930s, a gentle smile on her face. When I finished and rose to leave, she stretched out her arms and pulled me in for a hug. She whispered in my ear, "I am so grateful for you."

Choking back tears, I said, "I'm so grateful for you, Granny."

***

Christina Lyons continues to write freelance news on occasion, but primarily focuses on helping people write their memoirs, do genealogy research, and save their family history stories. Granny turned 102 in August of 2021.

47

Life Happens, and Then You Make It Happen
by Nancy Sharp

The day, June 17th, 2006, was a defining one. Widowed and twins in tow, this was the day I headed west to Denver. Life in New York City after eighteen years just wasn't worth the fast, noisy, people-populated-like-ants, cash-depleting, hassles-everywhere grind. Surviving the days was like a marathon, and I was worn out. I was conflicted and a bit sad about leaving behind family and friends, but the prospect of a different life, one that I could invent, was too fierce a gravitational pull to ignore. Moving to Colorado would be my Act II.

It had been a horrendous decade. My husband Brett was diagnosed with a brain tumor, though not the kind with a guaranteed death sentence. Because the tumor he had typically affects children ages five and under, and because a good percentage of those children survive, there was no way to predict Brett's prognosis. We prayed for the best, and for a good, long stretch, this seemed to be the case. It was against this calm backdrop that we decided to start a family since we were already in our mid-thirties and life was happening all around us. Unfortunately, on the very day that I delivered twins, a daughter, Rebecca, and a son, Casey, we learned the unimaginable: Brett's cancer had spread. The "routine" MRI he'd had the week prior, the one that had been clean for nearly two years, revealed tumors in his brain and down his spine. It was the worst possible news.

Brett hung on for a few more years but eventually lost his long battle to cancer in February of 2004. The kids weren't even three years old. In the end, his death was both anguishing and merciful.

I stayed put in New York City until the day came when I didn't think that I could handle one more month there. I was done with illness and mourning and just couldn't figure out how to stay in a place where despair blotted out any hope for the future. Was this really it for me—the life of a doomed widow at thirty-seven?

My moment of transformation came with little fanfare. While driving with my friend Lisa to visit my parents in Connecticut, I suddenly blurted out, "Why can't I just move to Colorado?" My college roommate, Julie, lived in Denver, and for years I'd dreamed of recasting my life in this city of sunshine, open skies, and towering mountains that could hold my gaze forever.

"You can," Lisa said. "What's stopping you?" She was so nonchalant in her reply that I might have been asking to go to the movies for the afternoon.

"Lisa, I can't just pick up and move to Denver. There's my parents and Brett's mom. I'd have to buy a house. Find new work. Find a school for the kids. Make friends. You know, how am I going to do all that?"

"You can do it," Lisa said, unfazed. "You absolutely can." She stared straight ahead.

This was a now-or-never moment. I saw it in the still composure on Lisa's face, how it reflected the longing in my heart. I'd conquered so many challenges; surely, I could manage one of my own choosing. Just like that, my decision was made. I'm not a runner and never will be, but the surge of energy I felt at that turnkey moment could have propelled me to run the New York City Marathon (the real one).

That's the upside of change: the adrenaline-pumping feeling of HOPE. Losing my husband to cancer changed my life forever but moving to Colorado gave me hope that a new story was possible.

Much has changed in the fifteen years since relocating to Denver, the place I call home. My children, now in college, are no longer children. And I'm remarried to a wonderful man named Steve whom I met through sheer serendipity and a little boldness, too.

About a year after moving to Denver, I read in the paper that Steve, a popular TV news anchor in Denver, had also lost his wife to cancer and was raising two teenage boys on his own. It so happened that Steve was being featured as one of the city's most eligible singles. *Why not?* I thought. *Why not write to him? What do I have to lose?*

We just celebrated thirteen years of marriage and have now officially entered the empty nest phase. Had I not taken a leap of blind hope by reaching out to Steve, I wouldn't have met the man I consider to be my soulmate—nor would Rebecca or Casey have a present father in their lives.

Life happens, and then you make life happen. These are the words I've come to live by and the greatest legacy, I believe, that I can pass along to my children and loved ones. Sadly, I lack the power to protect myself or my family from future pain—from unwelcome change, endings, and more loss. There will always be a million reasons not to do something when times get hard. These are the moments, the uneasy crossroads when resilience is forged. How we live matters. We might not always know the direction we're headed, but if we show up and put ourselves in the path of opportunity—even blind opportunity—we will forge forward.

***

Nancy Sharp holds an MFA in Creative Nonfiction and is the author of the memoir Both Sides Now: A True Story of Love, Loss, and Bold Living, *recipient of the Colorado Book Award. As a sought-after keynote speaker and trainer focused on resilience, Nancy presents to businesses and groups nationwide.*

48

Motivation from Degradation:
A Journey of Personal Success

by Lynette T. Noel

Monday class was four hours away, and I had been up a long while. Sleep eluded me, so I picked up one of the novels that I usually kept near my bed. After a few paragraphs, it lost its appeal, and I pushed it away. Television was not an option. It was too early for our only channel to begin transmission. I decided to start my devotions and get things going for the new week. Soon after, I rushed through breakfast and got ready to catch the 6:45 train to the city and then the quarter-mile walk to school with my friends. Yes, that was how I liked my days to go.

I came to our first class with all the excitement bubbling in me about the news I wanted to share with them—how I traveled from school the day before, waited some time to get the train, met my other traveling partners, and how we chatted about our escapades during the day. Real interesting stuff that fifteen-year-old students revelled in as we compared stories and tried to outdo each other. I had to tell them about the Nuts Man, who didn't always know the difference between salt nuts and fresh ones. We had to accept his mistake whether we liked what he gave us or not because he never refunded our money. Lots to share that morning. Dropping my bag, I gathered my group. "Girls, let me tell you this: Yesterday was something else."

That opened the door to a barrage of questions, comments, and the proverbial sounds of encouragement and intrigue. As it was Monday morning, each of us had a lot of good times to talk about since we met last Friday. "I'll go first." The others would have to wait until I told them about beach time with my family, falling asleep in church, hiding my younger sister's copybook, and forgetting to soak the red beans before cooking them. My weekend prepared me for the new week.

The school bell sounded, and we scampered to take up our position behind the singular wooden desks. The hum in the room faded to complete silence as we waited to join in with the Assembly Prayer. It seemed longer that morning, and I was anxious for it to end so I could continue with my weekend stories before classes began.

Miss Wally sauntered into our class and announced that we were going to review for the upcoming end-of-term test. I was not prepared for that. I certainly was not happy to postpone our girl chats until lunchtime, but at school, you had no choice but to obey the rules. We did just that. Miss Wally asked questions, choosing students at random to answer each one, and they seemed up to the task. When it was my turn, I did not hear the question and asked her to please repeat it. I knew she was not happy about that. She stared at me before moving on to continue the process of revision. At least I was spared an acid comment from her. My friends were not surprised about my action and how Miss Wally reacted.

I relaxed into the activities as, more and more, I saw the usefulness of the exercise as preparation for exams. I even forgot about the excitement for storytelling that had overtaken me before we began schoolwork. This was serious business, and I was glad to be there on time for it. The questions and the answers threw new light on those dark, unclear areas of that subject. Whole class revision had its benefits, after all. Miss Wally was certainly earning her salary!

With about twenty of us in class that day, and the session moving quickly, I was not surprised that Miss Wally pointed to me to answer another question. I don't remember what it was, but I do recall the scenario that unfolded. I had the displeasure of telling Miss Wally that I did not know the answer. That time, not only did she stare me down, as if I did not really exist, but her words affirmed her disgust for me: "Lynette T., for my part, you can go and rot!"

Have you ever been so startled that you convinced yourself that those words were not uttered to you? I summoned all my upbringing, and in true convent-style, I said, "Thank you, Miss." An internal monologue continued as I told myself that I was going to be a teacher, the best I could be, and I would never tell any of my students that. My classmates were quiet, stunned, and many refused to look at me – perhaps for fear that they, too, would be so maligned.

Why did I thank Miss Wally amidst the emotional turmoil that was raging in me? Years later, the answer to that was revealed. Unknown to her and my classmates, that was a turning point for me. The "class clown" became subdued, more focused on succeeding, and raised the bar on possibilities. No longer was I the person who got the privilege of attending one of the best girl-schools in my country and who enjoyed life with a passion and lacked true purpose. No. I was determined to prove Miss Wally wrong.

The journey to personal achievement had begun that morning with the silent promise to myself. I passed my subjects at Ordinary Levels, succeeded at Advanced Levels, and, in 1973, I attained my dream of becoming a primary school teacher. When I failed in that field, it was because of ignorance and not malice. I sought professional development whenever the opportunity arose—even if I had to fund it. My shelves were crowded with books and journals about reading, writing, and the art and science of teaching. I was determined to be the best. Former students came to me to recommend them to prospective employers. The emotional abuse endured at the hand of an "experienced" teacher became the catalyst that spurred me on.

Years later, as I look back on that day and the pain it caused, I realise that I had a choice to be perpetually engulfed in that degrading encounter or be propelled to a richer, more rewarding life of love and service. I nurtured students who excelled as assistant professors, principals, expert teachers, and prominent leaders in their spheres of accomplishment.

I did not rot.

The true meaning of my subservient "thank you" was revealed. I can now say, unreservedly and without malice, "Thank you, Miss Wally. Your push was painful, but it landed me on the pathway to success. Wherever you are, you will have to be proud of me. I am proud of who I have become."

***

Lynette T. Noel is a Senior Instructor in Reading at the University of Trinidad and Tobago and holds a Masters in Education from Mount Saint Vincent University. She is the author of The Bus Stories *and* The Night Nopat Was Left Out. *Her research interests are linguistic competence of struggling learners, adolescent literacy, and professional development for teachers. She is a doctoral student at the University of Trinidad and Tobago.*

49

The Red Plastic Cup

by Joanne McEnroy

*"Don't let it be forgot, that once there was a spot, for one
brief shining moment, that was known as Camelot."*
- Alan Jay Lerner, Camelot

When I was a child, summer did not officially begin until our annual trip to John's Bargain Store, the ubiquitous New York chain famous for its deeply discounted merchandise. We would shop its aisles and endcaps until our cart was filled with enough supplies to sustain us through all of July and August. We bought yellow sand pails, rubber flip flops, shorts, and tops. We also bought fly swatters, paper straws with swirly stripes, and our summer supply of plastic picnic cups and plates, which, for the next two months, my mother let us use for every inside meal as well. The cups came in packs of four, each one a different primary color, and, being as there was only one red cup in the pack, a great deal of angst and arguing ensued in our kitchen between my sister and me until my mother instituted a taped-to-the-refrigerator-turn-taking-chart-system. But, if she forgot to fill in that chart (which, more often than not, she did), I certainly did not remind her, which is how I always wrangled the lion's share of red cup use.

Summer was also the time of year when trucks, men, and machines would appear on our city street to repair the roads and sidewalks that were scarred by winter and just plain wear. They worked from just before we went outside to play in the morning until just before we were called back inside at the end of the day, breaking up sidewalks, curbs, and roads with picks and hammers swung wide and high over their heads. They mixed cement in large barrels and in trucks whose bellies turned slowly all day long. They spread shiny, hot tar with long-handled brooms, then flattened piles of gray pebbles on top of it before the hot asphalt trucks and steamrollers appeared to finish the job.

Their work was an inconvenience to fathers who were forced to park their cars on different blocks when they arrived home from work and to mothers who, laden with bags, had to crisscross their way around orange cones on their way home from shopping. But for every kid in the neighborhood, the work was nothing short of a miracle. How else would we ever have known what lurked beneath the streets and sidewalks upon which we had played for the entirety of our lives? We watched in awe all day as the men toiled, and in the evening, we scavenged tar-sticky treasures from the debris they'd left behind. As the summer days wore on, we made friends with these men from afar, and they laughed at our fascination with their work and at our foraging. But despite all of my watching, what never occurred to me—or, if it did, it held no particular significance—is that every single one of those men was Black. Which is why, at the end of one particularly hot summer day in August, my sister and I no longer had our red cup.

More than once that summer, my mother called me up to our apartment to carry down a pitcher of ice water that she prepared for the workmen. I would balance it, filled to the brim, and carry it down our long flight of stairs, out our door, across our stoop, and over our missing sidewalk. I would leave the pitcher on the curb and run back upstairs to get the sleeve of paper Dixie cups that my mother gave them to use for their drinks. But on one particular day, when I ran back up the stairs to get the Dixie cups, she instead handed me the cups that we used in our kitchen. They were stacked one inside the other, different sizes and colors, including our red cup, so that they made a tippy pile that I steadied as I made my way back down to the curb. It meant nothing to me at the time, giving the men these cups to use. And I supposed, if I supposed anything at all, that we were out of the paper ones. Mostly, I was just proud of the job I was doing and felt even prouder to be part of my mother's kindness. Other mothers weren't that thoughtful. They offered the men drinks from spigots on the side of their houses, if they offered them drinks at all. But my mother was nicer than that.

That evening, after all of the kids on the block were called inside for supper, and after we were scrubbed clean and sitting down at our own table to eat, I saw at each of our places winter glasses instead of the summer ones.

"Where's the red cup?" I asked, looking around the kitchen and at the chart on the refrigerator door. "Mom, the red cup? See? It's my turn."

But my mother did not answer me.

"Mom," I said again, "the red cup?"

"Don't worry about it," she said. "Just drink your milk and don't spill."

"But we want the *summer* cups," I said, this time enlisting my sister's help and hoping there was power in numbers. "Right?" and, as if on cue, my sister joined me in a sing-song chant. "Summer cups, summer cups, we want the summer…" but I stopped abruptly when I saw them sticking out of the garbage pail that stood in the corner of our kitchen. They were still stacked neatly, just the way the men had put them when they gave them back to me that very afternoon.

"Here they are!" I shouted as I jumped off my chair. But my mother's cry stopped me.

"No! Don't touch them," she shouted, then quietly, "They're dirty," she said. "They're dirty."

That didn't make sense to me, so I continued toward them, reaching into the pail. "But we can just put them in the sink and—"

"No!" she snapped. "Put them down. We can't. The workmen made them dirty." And then, as if she were trying to describe something final to a baby, she whispered, "They, they are broken."

I thought maybe she was about to cry, so I held up the stack of cups and turned to face her. "But they aren't broken, Mom. See? We just have to wash them!" But some of my confidence slipped away as I stood, staring into her face.

I waited for her to answer, but she didn't, until tears welled up in my eyes, too.

"The men made them too dirty to wash," she said, hoarse and throaty. Then she turned her head away from me and looked down at her plate.

Suddenly, as if renewed, she looked up and said, "I have an idea. We can get new cups! We'll go to the Avenue tomorrow and buy them. I promise. And these cups? These cups can be for the men when we give them water tomorrow."

I dropped the stack back into the pail and stared at her. From somewhere deep inside, a cold realization, primeval almost, began to plague me.

"It's mean," I finally said to her. "It's mean to only pretend to be nice."

I walked out of the room, toward the front of the house, where I stared out the window at the empty street below. I surveyed the remnants of the work the men had done that day, saw the rubble piles, the smoothly asphalted edges, the still broken sidewalks, the new curbs. The street was empty and quiet. Broken, yet new. It mirrored the way I felt inside. When she called me to come back into the kitchen, I did not go. And, uncharacteristically, my mother did not make me. I remained at that window until it was too dark to see, except for the street lamps casting blue shadows, but I imagined the daytime, the sunlight, the happiness that I had felt just a few hours before. It was gone now.

We had come to a new understanding that night, my mother and me, an understanding for which I had not yet found the words. But this much I knew. I no longer felt proud, and I could not explain why. Or perhaps, I had. *It was mean to only pretend to be nice.*

***

Joanne McEnroy is happily retired from teaching. A Guided Autobiography student for the past two years, she continues to meet and write with her original GAB group. "They have become, along with my husband, my inspiration to keep it going." A recently trained instructor, she now has the joy and privilege of facilitating new Guided Autobiography groups on Long Island, New York.

50

The Coins Clink Clank

by Sara Mei Woo

The coins clink, clank as I drop them onto the tin can. "Ma, look! Po-po, again, paid in one-cent coins! She took so long to count them, one by one! Well, at least she poured the curry noodles onto her own bowl and I need not return to collect our bowl when she's eaten them.

"Ma, why do you give Po-po more noodles, more cockles, more pig's blood pudding, more cuttlefish, more bean sprouts, and more dried bean curd puff?"

"Shhhh… quiet!" Ma is annoyed at my continuous complaint. "Po-po is old and she saved up the coins so she can buy herself a bowl of noodles that she enjoys. You have to be patient, young girl! And remember, be understanding!"

Mama is very much an entrepreneur. She's got no choice but to take on the role of breadwinner for the family. Pa-pa had been fiercely independent as a carpenter, working on local building projects or bringing workers to the other States. But Pa-pa suddenly had fallen ill and had been hospitalized. With no income, Ma started her food business.

I had to grow up instantly, as I'm the eldest and my two brothers are very much younger. I walk daily to the hospital to see Pa-pa, bringing him food before going to school.

During the weekdays, I sell Ma's fried rice vermicelli and noodles with the help of a kind neighbor. We live in our "kampong," a community of neighbors within the compound. Many families stay within this compound in their individual homes. It's safe for us children to play within the compound. Interestingly, we have a neighbor rearing chickens, and another has an aviary. I now have no time to play, only time to sell my fried noodles after school.

I've never forgotten this period of time when I spent my weekends helping my Ma-ma to peddle the streets, selling our scrumptious curry noodles—delicious!

Ma-ma is right; I learned to be more conscious and patient with Po-po when she counts her coins, clink clank!

One day, I met a very kind lady, she talked to me caringly, asking about my school and family. I looked forward to bringing the noodles to her house and getting to see the two kor-kor (older brothers). So handsome!

Ma said to me one day, "You stay here, I'm taking this bowl of noodles to the uncle who ordered."

Ma came back with the noodles. "Ma, why do you still have the noodles?"

"He's not there." Mother knew best; she had a hunch and did not send me. In those days, children were abducted. I felt blessed and well protected.

It was early February 1965; Ma and I were out peddling our delicious curry noodles. A car stopped by us. A modern, well-dressed, pretty lady stepped out, and Ma looked surprised! I've not seen her... who is she? Ma says, "Call her Auntie Peng! Auntie Peng, my sister, she just arrived from Singapore!"

At home, Auntie Peng told Ma and Pa to move to Singapore so Pa could see a good eye doctor. Pa's left eye had become badly infected during his illness and had to be removed. He had a false glass eye fitted.

His right eye was affected, but he could still see. By moving to Singapore to see an eye specialist, Pa could save his only eye.

Quick decision, quick action! Within the next two weeks, Ma and Pa sorted out the things that could be sold, given away, or taken with us. We were booked to leave on February 28th, eight days after my tenth birthday.

I'm so sad; leaving my hometown meant I wouldn't see my school friends, teachers, and the neighbor's children with whom we played marbles, shuttle, hop-scotch. The best was climbing up the neighbors' trees to pluck our favorite fruits, guava and chiku. At night, we climbed up the trees to catch fireflies. I was proud to be the only girl climbing up the tree with the boys while the rest of the girls held a bottle, waiting for us to catch the fireflies and come down to put them into the bottles. The fun, triumph, and strength climbing up to catch the fireflies and down the tree set in me an attitude and mindset: we can do what we want if we act on it! This set forth my life and career as I was growing up.

A week before we left, I told Pa and Ma that I wanted to talk to them. "Is it something troubling you?" Pa asked.

"Yes, Pa!"

Ma wasn't happy; she was busy sorting out our belongings. "What is it now?" Ma asked.

"I want to stay in Penang. Pa, Ma, and brothers can all move to Singapore."

Pa asked, "Where are you going to stay?"

"Here in this room!" I said innocently. The house where we had stayed had three rooms, and there was an open space in front of the house.

"What about your food?"

"Pa, you can give me the money, and I will ask our neighbor to cook food for me!" Totally naïve, but independent thinking!

The day arrived, neighbors came, we said goodbyes, and we went to the train station to start our journey going south towards a new and unfamiliar state—Singapore!

It was night; I was the only one awake. "Dubdubdubdubdubdub," the hypnotic sound of the train. Feeling sad, missing my school and friends. There was moonlight shining in the cabin. It was beautiful, a sense of warmth came over me. I walked to the corridor and saw the moonlight shining on the vast fields of green. A sense of peace came over me. I realized there was no turning back, and onward we must go to seek a new life!

My family arrived in Singapore in the wee hours on March 1st, 1965. Auntie Peng and her husband were there to meet us. Wow, a beautiful, big blue car to pick us up!

The car vroomed to life, and we were on our way. I looked out of the window, the sun's rays warmed my face. And I prayed, "May we all live a happy life in this new city."

Today, we can all say it was the right choice that the family moved south to Singapore.

***

Sara Mei Woo is a certified GAB Instructor, Certified Laughter Yoga Teacher, Laughter Ambassador, and Life Transition Consultant. A volunteer for four decades and advisor to a local Asia-Pacific women's organization, she created Project Taking Charge, a program for women in shelters. Sara lives in Singapore, where she brings laughter, yoga, and joy to seniors.

51

The Train Ride to Vivian
by Vivian Clecak

"Home" was sitting on a high stool, listening to my mother's favorite soap operas and watching her roll out dough for a special bread. My dad was an invalid, our family sad in many ways, and my mother was my comfort, my safe place.

I became my mother's comfort child as I grew older. I wrote her sweet notes, and I brought home awards and prizes in the way a puppy brings home bones.

I was a star student and won a full scholarship to Stanford University. As the youngest of two children, I had been the light of my parent's life since my sister left for college three years earlier. My mother was incredibly proud of me.

She wanted me to go to Stanford and have all the exciting opportunities possible. I would have stayed and gone to a local university if she had asked. She did not ask.

The day came when I was leaving for Stanford. My father did not go out much as my mom had to push him in the wheelchair up and down curbs. But she brought him to the train station; he wanted to be there to see me off to my new beginning.

One of the hardest moments of my life was climbing the stairs to the train and watching my mother standing behind the wheelchair and my dad leaning forward to wave. They looked so small.

I did not go directly to Palo Alto. I went first to Los Angeles to spend a few days with my sister at UCLA. Finally, it was time for me to actually go to college.

My name is Dvera Vivian. My mother had chosen the name Deborah after the Hebrew priestess noted in the Old Testament. But for some reason, she spelled my secular name as Dvera. Teachers could not pronounce it; kids made fun of it, "Dvera, diarrhea."

My family called me Vivi; my friends called me Vivian. Dvera was a shy, quiet, very serious student. Vivi and Vivian were lively, fun, silly, not so afraid.

Getting on the train, I made the decision to become Vivian, to introduce myself to new friends as Vivian.

The train from LA was filled with Stanford students. The first person I met on the train was a good-looking guy, older than me for sure, who offered me a drink from a small bottle he was carrying. The only alcohol I had ever tried was sweet wine on Jewish holidays, but Vivian was up for the new experience. It burned going down my throat.

The good-looking guy moved on. I had not been able to keep the conversation going. Dvera was still shy.

I was so nervous, excited, scared, expectant on that train ride. I could not wait to get there. Vans from the housing service met us at the station and took us to our dorms. I met a few girls in the van, and we all agreed we would meet later in the dorm dining hall for dinner.

I come from a religious Jewish home. My parents were JEWISH. It was the center of their lives. We always fasted on Yom Kippur, the holiest day of the year. My father used to say he would have killed himself if it were not for his faith.

I met my new friends to walk together to the dining hall. This was my first day, my first dinner at Stanford, and it happened to be Yom Kippur. I had already made the decision to eat dinner, as part of my new beginning.

Dinner was formal. We were seated and served at our small tables. The first course was a delicious, tangy salad. It did not taste familiar. I asked one of the girls what the salad was.

Ham Salad.

Vivian had arrived at her new life.

***

Vivian Clecak has been a seeker for much of her life. She is an activist, feminist, psychotherapist, founder of a domestic violence program, loving wife and mother, widow, and grief support counselor. The experience of leading Guided Autobiography groups has deepened her commitment to being a compassionate support and witness.

52

Cloud Nine

by Janice Bauder

Dreams. Expectations. Hope for the future. Still single and approaching thirty, my dream of being married, along with the expectation of having children and the hope of growing old with someone at my side, was becoming a figment of my active imagination. However, while I was filling my life with work, taking college classes in the evening and volunteering, my mother was keeping the vision alive by suggesting I attend a weekend singles conference at Concordia University in Ann Arbor, Michigan.

Somewhat reluctantly, I found myself hopping into my Mercury Marquis the day after my twenty-ninth birthday for the forty-five-minute drive to the singles conference. I told myself it would be a nice little get-away, and I would enjoy attending the sessions and hearing the messages. However, as I was getting ready to attend the first session on Friday night, I put on my royal blue sundress, curled my hair, and walked in with a million-dollar smile just in case someone was looking!

As an icebreaker, the speaker passed out paper and tape and asked that we attach the paper to our backs. We were asked to introduce ourselves to one another and then write a positive comment on the paper based on our first impression. When I turned to look at the person behind the rich-as-chocolate voice that said, "Someone wrote something nice about you," I saw his blue eyes and round face for the first time. As we exchanged superficial niceties, I concluded he was a seminary student and somewhat serious but worth pursuing nonetheless.

When Saturday morning rolled along, I adjusted my objective to not only fully engage in the sessions of the day but seek out opportunities to talk with the "seminary student." To my dismay, our paths did not cross during the session portion of the day. I was not discouraged, however, as I was filled with rich teaching and practical life application, receiving it without being distracted.

Life is full of making adjustments here and there, so my next plan was to sit at his table for dinner. The problem was, I didn't see him at dinner. I tweaked the plan again and thought, surely, I would see him at the square dance that night. He was there, in the group right next to mine. After a short break, he was gone, and I did not see him anymore that evening.

With resignation in my spirit, I decided to go to the chapel and pray. As I entered the stained-glass-lined sanctuary, I felt as if I was stepping on holy ground as the Presence of God surrounded me. I bowed at the altar and prayed, giving thanks for all that I had learned that day, asking for help to apply the principles. Finally, my prayer was, "Lord, I have been trying all day to meet this guy. Tomorrow is the last day of the conference. Please provide a way for me to meet him."

Having rested well Saturday night and feeling somewhat casual Sunday morning, I put on my aqua blue and white striped shirt with coordinating capris and headed to breakfast. I had just finished up when I saw him coming toward me carrying his breakfast tray. He asked if the seat next to me was taken. Inwardly, I thought, *Thank you, Jesus*, while outwardly, I flashed a smile and warmly invited him to have a seat.

We talked for a few minutes. I learned that his name was Jim, and he was not a seminary student. Rather, he lived in Lafayette, Indiana, and worked for the State of Indiana. I started to get up to dispose of my dirty dishes, and Jim said, "It was nice meeting you," to which I replied, "Oh, I am coming back!" We spent the rest of our time there attending the worship service together and exchanging addresses.

I inhabited Cloud Nine for the next seven months as we corresponded through letters, phone calls, and monthly visits. It was during this time that I learned Jim was not naturally serious. In fact, his dry sense of humor and limitless supply of puns provided a steady stream of belly laughs.

When the marriage proposal came on February 21st, 1986, it was with the understanding that I would move to Lafayette, Indiana, from my Sterling Heights, Michigan home. With my head still firmly planted in the fluffy white clouds, we chose September 13th to tie the knot.

As the time got closer, I began the descent into reality. Yes, I loved this man, but I was leaving the place that had been my home for thirty years, a very good job, discontinuing my pursuit of a college degree, leaving extended family…everything familiar for a man with whom I had not spent consistent time.

I knew there was only one place I could go that would bring closure to my single life, and that was a visit to my rock in Lexington, Michigan.

Every summer, my friend Toni and I would spend a week at my Aunt Bert's home near the shores of Lake Huron. In 1972 we walked along the beach until we reached two rocks set side-by-side sitting up out of the water. We would spend hours there talking over the gentle sound of waves slapping playfully against the rocks. We painted our names on the rocks and returned to have more rich conversations the next year, and the next.

A week before the wedding, I headed up to Lexington for the day. It was bright and sunny, not a cloud in the sky. I slipped off my sandals before entering the private beach. The cool sand squeezed through my toes as I walked along the shoreline, eagerly anticipating a visit to my coveted rock. Was it still there?

To my delight, I could see it from a distance and ran the rest of the way! As I climbed up onto the rock named "Jan, '72," enveloped in the light of the warm sun, I couldn't help but break out in praise for the assurance I felt at that moment. This fork in the road was indeed a gift from the Lord. As I looked out over the water where the whitecaps coming into the shore looked like delicate lace, I prayed, "Lord, you are giving me a new life, and I don't know what to expect, but because you answered my prayer in that chapel, I know you have ordained this, and I can trust you with it."

It has been nearly thirty-five years since He fulfilled my dream of being married and having children, giving me grandchildren as a bonus. My prayer in the chapel, offered while seeing filtered light through the beautiful stained glass windows, was answered by the true unfiltered Light of the World. While my earthly rock has crumbled and deteriorated, the Solid Rock is the eternal firm foundation and worthy to be trusted, particularly in any life crossroad I encounter.

***

Janice is married to Jim, a mother of two and one daughter-in-love, and known as Grandma Hobbit to Miles and Shiloh. Janice recently moved to Fate, Texas. Her passion is encouraging people to value their life stories, and she anticipates continuing her "Your Story Matters - Tell It!" GAB workshops in North Texas.

53

Toss the Biscuit

by Christine Roski

I looked around, and all I saw were unremarkable memories of my childhood. The kitchen in which almost every meal in my twenty-one years had been shared, the old refrigerator that never had enough ice cubes, and the blue dishes were still here. But there I sat, cross-legged under the kitchen table, snuggled up against my old dog, crying.

I was alone, trying to make some sense of the choices that had brought me to this unsettling situation. Everything in my life had been so normal, so predictable. Then came the call that sent my life veering off its road of comfortable boredom.

After graduating from Nazareth College of Rochester, I had moved back to Fairport, New York, and planned on working to put myself through grad school. My History degree hadn't proven very marketable. Plan B was to get my teaching credential, something that felt within my reach. I began looking for work but soon found that I was either over-qualified or under-qualified for just about every job in town. The people I talked to were kind but agreed that I just wasn't a fit for any of their positions. I needed money, and the rent was due. Finally, the temp agency called about an opening as a bank teller. My future was looking brighter.

Well, that bright light began to dim quickly. I seemed to be the only one left trying to balance out every night. I always managed to get the same miserable people in my line, and I really wasn't sorry when the manager, in the kindest way possible, told me that banking just wasn't meant for me.

A few days later, a friend called from New York City to offer me a job where she worked. The job didn't pay much, and it was only for one year at the most. All I needed to do was run their small office. I had no experience running anything, let alone an office, but it wasn't the bank, and it was NYC! How difficult could it be? Two days later, I had my ticket to La Guardia.

That's how this whole thing started. I was going to New York City with fifty dollars in my purse, one new dress, and absolutely no idea what my new job would demand. But I was finally on my adventure, headed for the Big Apple!

Things happened quickly. I moved into an apartment in Greenwich Village with my friend from the office. Actually, I was told that my room was the little alcove next to the front room. It came with an outdoor lounge chair which would be my bed, and a window. Again, things were looking up.

Within a few weeks, I was jumping on and off subways, ordering from the deli like a true New Yorker, and falling in love. I hadn't planned on the love part.

He was this amazing guy from Oklahoma who worked in our office. We went to the Statue of Liberty, and I liked the way he held my hand. We set out to conquer the city. We walked all around Central Park and bought hot dogs from the street vendors. Every morning he would come into our office with a cup of hot chocolate and a warm bagel. He would place them on my desk and smile at me. I had never received such treasures. When he made room for my toothbrush next to his, I knew things were getting serious.

Things were really heating up, putting my future plans into question. Every walk seemed to bring us into another deep discussion. We argued about religion, had heated discussions about our future and his girlfriend – did I mention his girlfriend in Germany, who was somehow still in the picture? Needless to say, we talked about her a lot. And along the way, we fell in love.

Fast forward to a convention in Atlanta. I was out to prove that I was not ready for a serious commitment. I tried my hardest to make him upset with me. I was moody and defiant, and it seemed to be working. Then he came into our little office at the convention and insisted we go outside for a walk. I went reluctantly, knowing that it might be our last walk together. Then he did it. He didn't say one word. He merely took his glass of Coke and threw it across the parking lot. I had never seen such a pass in my life, and I had never seen anyone so hurt. Maybe it was just frustration. Regardless, the message was clear – I was more than important to this man. He wasn't going to just give up on me, on us.

In fairy tales, they might say that my prince had finally come. He had risked it all to win me, to gather me into his arms and promise me a life full of red balloons. All the birds were singing. I knew we would be together forever, and we would figure things out along the way.

In just six weeks, we were married. That was it, "my life" was now "our life," and we were moving away from New York. Soon after our wedding, I began to throw up a lot, and it seemed that we were taking someone else on our new adventure. Things kept happening very fast.

We drove to Oklahoma to await his orders from the Air Force, stopping in my hometown to say goodbye.

So here I am, sitting on the floor under my parent's kitchen table, wondering how all this came about. I can't even look into my dog's eyes as he kisses my arm because I know that, if I do, I will really lose it. My goodbyes to my parents have all been finished and my new husband is waiting in the car to start our journey west. I asked for a minute to check things once more, and now it was time to leave.

So why am I crying? This place has never really been a place of warmth and love. The table was a place where we usually sat in silence, eating our meals. Maybe that is part of the problem. I am searching for wonderful memories, special moments of time that I can remember and hold on to as I begin my new life. Nothing, just my dear old dog kissing my arm.

Time to leave, he's honked the horn, and I know we have to get to St. Louis tonight. One last look, and I feel a rush of excitement fill me up. I know someday I will come back to this house, I will eat breakfast at this table, and the refrigerator will never have enough ice cubes. That's all ahead of me, I am ready to wipe my tears away and kiss that old dog. I toss him a biscuit and run out the door.

***

Christine Roski grew up outside of Rochester, New York, watching the Mickey Mouse Club and dreaming of Southern California. Faith and family have always been the central core of her life. Chris loves reading, visiting with her twelve grandchildren, and going on walks with her forever friend and husband, Ray.

54

Jose

by Jean Stumpf

Between my job as a medical records auditor and pharmacy technician during the late nineties, I took a time-out to rejuvenate my spirits and evaluate my career. Burned out and disillusioned by the nursing home industry and the health care world in general, I felt I deserved a break. Not having any job skills outside of health care and needing to pay my rent, I landed a job at a local Safeway grocery store as a cashier.

When I told my mother about my job change, her first reaction (I kid you not) was, "Oh my god, now I will have to start being nice to the clerks at the Jewel!"

"What a horrible thing to say, mother!" I retorted.

"Well, Jean Ann, you know what I mean. Why would you waste your precious time on that? Any nincompoop could do that job."

I remember telling her how, for a little while, I just wanted a job where I couldn't possibly kill anyone.

"The worst thing I can do on this job is overcharge or undercharge a customer," I said.

At the end of each shift, I would punch out and not worry what undone work I was leaving behind or wonder if I committed an unrecognized serious error with life-threatening consequences. This was the freedom I was looking for during this break in my health care career.

When I started my job at the grocery store, the work felt easy. I never felt I was working hard enough. Safeway emphasized customer service, and I did whatever I could to meet the company's mission. Service with a smile. Go that extra mile. Thank everyone using their name. The way I performed, you would think I was vying for a management position.

I appreciated and liked this cashier job. Following the company script never bothered me. I put on a happy face, and soon enough, I would be feeling happy no matter what mood I started with. Didn't all employees feel like me? *And if not, why not?* I often asked myself. There was no job stress for me at this place.

One day I went to my car on a lunch break. As I walked through the parking lot, I saw Jose, a courtesy clerk, crouching between two cars with his head bowed down. He was eating something. It seemed to me he was hiding. In an instant, I resented him for being a lazy slacker, hiding out there instead of collecting and bringing all the used shopping carts back to the front of the store.

No wonder our customers were complaining! I thought to myself. I made a mental note to report what I had seen to Joe, the front-end manager.

I cornered Joe in the break room.

"Joe, you really need to talk to Jose," I said. "He's out there hiding between the cars when he is supposed to be doing cart duty." My indignation was loud and clear.

"Let me tell you about Jose," Joe said in his even-toned voice. "He's out there eating mayonnaise sandwiches on day-old white bread. He takes the mayo packets from the deli. I give him the expired bread. This is his second job. He's already worked a graveyard shift at Home Depot."

Joe stopped a second, took a deep breath, then said, "Did you know he sends most all of his money back to his family in Mexico? It's time for you to get back to work."

Then he walked out of the break room.

My face burned red. With shame.

After lunch, when I returned to my assigned cash register, I saw Jose standing there waiting to bag the groceries that traveled down my conveyor belt. His eyes were half-closed. I saw deep wrinkles furrowing his brow. I saw his scuffed-up leather shoes, worn thin – even on their tops, where his toes were. I could see his white socks peeking through.

I was so mad at myself for being a tattletale. I was grateful to Joe, my manager, for being so direct with me.

Imagine the unrecognized luxury at this time in my life – to be able to choose a job, thinking it would give me a break from the high stress I had been feeling. What a privilege to consider a particular job as a recovery period. Jose, crouched between the cars, was just as entitled to his recovery period as I was.

My unquestioned assumption saw Jose crouched between cars in a manner far from his reality. Far from the truth.

I had not given a person in that workspace any consideration or benefit of my doubt. The burning feeling inside me was a helpful shame. I am trying to notice when feelings like these arise in me. Pseudo guilt and shame feelings can be tools to help me discover and uncover unconscious biases I have and how they inform my judgments of others.

Joe and Jose taught me that people have unique stories, coping strategies, and life stresses I don't know about or even could imagine. Best to withhold my judgments or be quiet about them until I consider how I might not understand another person's circumstances.

Writing and sharing my stories, like this one, with a trusted group has helped me uncover and re-frame many events in my life. Like a new eyeglass prescription – I didn't realize what I was missing until I saw things through new lenses.

***

Jean Stumpf has participated in life story legacy writing groups since 2012. After completing the Birren Center for Autobiographical Studies instructors course, she has led writing groups using GAB themes, prompts, and methods at senior centers, libraries, nursing homes, bookstores, in private homes, and online.

55

If You Love Her, Let Her Go

by Lori Stokan Smith

I hold on to her for dear life. The smell of car exhaust is ripe in the clogged air. Monday, March 28th, 2016, is an overcast, gray day at bustling Chicago O'Hare Airport. Noise engulfs us. Airplane engines roar above. A taxi swooshes to the next fare. Car doors slam. Luggage wheels creak under their load. Malingering airport workers trade friendly banter. Unemotional activity and perfunctory routine envelopes us all around.

We hug in the middle of the sooty sidewalk. She pats my back, probably thinking *The other students on the bus are all looking. Time to let go, Mom.* I don't want to let go.

I hold on for one long second more. Knowing I have pushed the limits of her mood, I put on a stoic face and release her from my mother's grip. I hear the words inside my head, *If you love her, let her go.* The bus that will carry her back to college is lined up at the curb of the Bus Shuttle Center. She has already stowed her backpack emblazoned with "Chargers #13," a holdover of her high school life.

We say our goodbyes, both equally sad. Maybe I was the only one who felt relief that this was a good visit, having parted on bad terms on two prior visits. I, not quite understanding the reason for the rift, and she, believing with all her heart and soul the merits of her rightness and of her mother's complete and total wrongness.

Now she walks up the stairs into the abyss of the bus. To avoid embarrassing my daughter, I walk past the end of the Motor Coach bus until the other college returnees cannot see me if they, by chance, glance up from their cell phones. There I stop and turn, just to look. I walk a little further and turn again. I hesitate and glance one last time—one last chance for connection. One last chance to hold on. The scene reminds me of a long-ago memory.

Christmas 1982 was over. I was commencing my first trip back to college on my own. I had only traveled once before to West Point. Six months earlier, I had been in the secure cocoon of our family car with my mother and brother Ed, having traveled eight hours from home to start Beast Barracks, the first six weeks of demanding physical and mental challenges at the United States Military Academy at West Point. This time, I was flying from Pittsburgh to New York. From the airport, I had to find a bus that would take me to Port Authority and then to Grand Central Station in the heart of New York City. Once there, I had to find a bus that would take me to West Point. I did all this transferring while carrying a heavy, over-packed suitcase. It is important to note that back in January 1983, the hoi polloi [1] did not have access to the internet, with its wealth of information, or, for the most part, luggage with wheels. I had no cell phone either. Like Mary Tyler Moore, I had to make it on my own. To raise my stress level and exhaustion quota even higher, West Point required "plebes" (first-year cadets) to travel in "dress gray"— a traditional wool uniform that cinched its priest-like collar around my jugular and allowed for little free movement.

At eighteen, I had never navigated New York City before, and this was not a good introduction. Feeling like everyone was staring at me in my uniform and not seeing any other cadet, I followed the masses when the bus dumped me at the Port Authority. I asked one authority figure after another, " How do I…? Where do I….? How much is…? What time is…?" I did not own a credit card, and debit cards wouldn't be popular for another decade. I hoped I had enough cash on hand to cover the bus ticket. I vividly recall standing in the aptly named Grand Central Station and asking a big, round-bellied Irish Customer Service Agent with rosy cheeks where I should go. Like most people back then, he seemed amused by this little girl in uniform who did not know, as my dad used to say, "sh-t from Shinola"[2] but one day, most likely would.

I remember the smell of gasoline, the fumes from the lined-up buses, and the waiting drivers. I checked and rechecked that I had the right ticket and the right bus—once, twice, and, still not being certain, a few times more. I remember the feeling of relief when I was finally sitting on the bus headed to West Point. Sweat poured off my forehead from where my uniform saucer hat rubbed too tightly. A drop of sweat slowly streamed down the small of my back as the sun poured its heat into the bus window. The bus door closed. But the relief of successfully navigating from home quickly faded as I shifted gears to focus on what lay ahead: new semester, new schedule, new squad leader, plebe duties, memorizing the menus for the day, shining my shoes, getting yelled at…

As I stood at the O'Hare bus station, looking at the backside of the bus my daughter was sitting on, I felt like history was repeating itself. Now my little girl was having to become an adult. She had always deferred to me to ask questions of the people in charge. Now she was the one asking the customer service representative if her ticket was good for the express bus. She was now the one confirming with the driver that this was the bus to Notre Dame. I was happy to be there, to coax her to ask the questions. I was happy she did ask. I was happy she was growing with each question she asked, with each transfer she made, and each journey she conquered. I knew how complicated and dirty and exhausting it all was, this process of growing up. I remember the feeling of wanting to be independent but still wanting to be coddled. Now, as a mother, I, too, was growing. Parenting adolescents is hard. Letting go is harder. The bus was pulling away. *If you love her, let her go.*

***

Lori Stokan Smith is a Birren Certified Guided Autobiography Instructor and published author. She is a member of the Bloomingdale Writers

Connection, where she co-teaches Life Story Writing Classes and facilitates a monthly writing group, The Story Tellers. An Army veteran, she helped fight the Cold War in West Germany and later became a military spouse, a mother, and a committed volunteer. Writing is her passion.

---

1. hoi polloi = the masses, the common people; expression from Greek meaning "many" or "the people."

2. You don't know "Sh*t from Shinola" = A colloquialism which dates back to the early 1940s in the United States, sometimes ended with "that's why your shoes don't shine." Shinola was a popular brand of shoe polish, which had a color and texture not unlike feces. As a verb, it means to not have even the most basic level of intelligence or common sense.

56

Moments That Stay With Me

by John Countryman

W hat an adventure parenting can be. Oh, the things we discover about ourselves, about life. And the crossroad we all know is coming—someday.

I felt pretty sheepish, to be honest. My wife was creating a masterpiece. It was a quilt, the sort that becomes an attractive wall hanging rather than a bedroom accessory. The quilt was a patchwork of variegated batik fabrics—rich umbers, resplendent greens, pointillist textures— representing the tree of life, an image especially meaningful to my daughter, tattooed as it is across her back, and emblazoned on her wedding invitations.

As I watched the quilt-making in progress, I fretted about how inadequate my own gift might be by comparison. How do you match an item so thoughtful, so personalized, so creative, so loving, when you've never (at least, to your own mind) been one to create anything material and original by hand as my wife was doing, one perfect painstaking piece at a time. Was I to get my daughter and her husband-to-be a Hamilton Beach electric mixer? Do they still make those? Is it Kitchen Aid now? How predictable and uninspired!

I was moved and awed by how absorbed my wife appeared in her work as a master fabric artist, and I was just a little jealous. I tried to recall an occasion in my own life when a creative activity had engaged me in the same way but came up empty again and again. Until, in a flash of insight, I remembered writing some poetry as an undergraduate in imitation of my older brother, also a student at the college and one of the editors of handcrafted rag-paper chapbooks distributed to teachers, family, and friends. I certainly didn't consider myself a poet in the professional sense (and I still don't), but I recalled that I was reasonably good at it.

So, given my wedding gift dilemma and a desire to bring "the personal touch" to the occasion, I determined to take another stab at free verse and author a book of poetry for my betrothed only child and her beau.

For inspiration, I turned to our family albums filled with photos of my daughter from the day of her birth to the most recent "selfies" I cribbed from her social media posts. (We called it, in jest, our "shrine" to Sarah.) And my strategy worked. I was able to produce a book (acid-free linen this time) of thirteen poems I was *reasonably* happy with—not New Yorker magazine worthy, but not embarrassing, either.

The photos—and thus the poems—began with the very first captures when I shot an entire roll of (are you ready?) DOUBLE-EXPOSED images, the first-ever of our newborn, because I mindlessly loaded the same film in the camera twice. Since the only "camera" Sarah has ever known is a feature on her cell phone, she finds this incident deeply amusing! How crushed I'd been when the photos were returned, and I discovered my mistake—and how I treasure those photos now! The visual history of my daughter's life in the several albums we've assembled ranged from photos of my wife holding her as a toddler right up to her college graduation.

Curiously, it was one poem that was not prompted by a photo that surprised me, and about which I am most satisfied. Poring over the several albums provoked other memories for which there are no Kodachrome images—except the ones in my head. Memories that brought a smile to my face and tugged at my heart. One of them, my fondest, was when Sarah was transitioning to her own bedroom. Following the obligatory bedtime oration of "If I Ran the Circus," she wanted us to stay beside her until she fell asleep. Needless to say, *that* was a nightly adventure! And as I brought forth the poetic re-imagining of those precious hours and minutes in my own and my daughter's life, as I felt the sense of an ending, I was surprised by what came out of my mouth, out of my mind, out of my pen, onto the page. And I wept.

This is that poem.

STAY WITH ME
Once upon a time,
At bedtime,
Every time
It came time
To slip away so you could sleep,
You'd say:
"Stay with me!"
A little panic in your voice.

And so, I would.
I'd stay with you.

And I'd be sure
You'd drifted off.
Or so I thought!
But, no!
The instant I began to leave your room:
"Stay with me!"
You weren't sleeping after all.
"Stay with me!"

And so, I would.
I'd stay with you.

Many nights the minutes passed,
Hours sometimes,
Until you'd drift away, and I could go.

But I would listen
Right next door
And sometimes you would call.
"Where'd you go?"
And I'd return.
"Stay with me."

And so, I would.
I'd stay with you.

In time you came to trust
That I'd be there.
That you could rest
Assured that "staying"
Also meant "nearby."
Not far away.
You weren't alone.

Never worry.
I know you want me close
Even now—
Even now when time and space
Are greater than
The steps I took
To reach the room next door.

I know it;
I know
You want to have me stay with you…
Still.

When we're apart.
When there's a "here" and "there."
When I am "here," and you are "there."

And…

When I'm no longer "here" at all.

"Stay with me!"
And so, I will.
I'll stay with you.
Now close your eyes.
The dreams will come.

***

John Countryman, 72, is a retired theatre professor in an encore career as a gerontologist. He currently serves as Lifelong Learning Coordinator for the Shepherd's Center of Richmond, Virginia. John is a Certified Guided Autobiography Facilitator, Certified Reminiscence and Life Review Practitioner, Narrative4 Story Exchange Facilitator, and Life Story Theatre Facilitator.

57

A New England Girl

by Ruth McCully

S ometimes you find yourself in a place, a town, a city, or a part of
the country, and you know deep in your core that you are home.
That is how it is with me. I am a New England Girl. When I am in New
England, I am at peace, and deep in my heart's core, I know I am home. I
belong here. It is a good feeling.

I was born in Boston and raised in a small town not far from there.
Norwood, Massachusetts, was the lens through which I first experienced
the world. Some would call it a sheltered life. I call it idyllic, safe, and
home.

We lived on Everett Avenue, a street where each house was different,
two stories and old, but not very old. I walked everywhere. I walked to
Winslow Elementary School and walked home for lunch. My brothers
and my father came home for lunch, too. We ate together, and then we
walked back to school, and my dad went back to work at the Alice Gift
Shop on Washington Street. Sometimes, my mother would take us all
food shopping at the Star Market, and we would walk there and back,
carting our groceries in my brother's red wagon. We had one car, a station
wagon, which my father drove.

Down the street and around the corner was Franniolli's, a corner store.
Every neighborhood had a corner store. My mother would send me to
Franniolli's to pick up milk, bread, hamburger, and sometimes Oleo. She
always called it "Oleo" instead of margarine. She would have to teach me

how to say Oleo because, by the time I got to the store, I would forget how to pronounce it. Mrs. Franniolli did not know what I was looking for when I called it "OleyOley." It was always better when my mother sent a note with me. Franniolli's was a one-room store with wooden floors, wooden shelves that lined the walls, and glass cases that contained penny candy. I particularly liked Mary Janes.

I loved the seasons and the changes that came with them. When it snowed, we would go to the Bond Street playground for sledding, and we could sled non-step for several blocks through the park from Washington Street to Main Street. We used old candles to wax the runners of the sleds, and we went fast. In the summer, we took swimming lessons for our Red Cross cards at the municipal pool, played at the playground, and when it was really hot, we kids would sleep on the screened-in front porch. We always went to the same place for vacation. Each summer, we would drive eight hours through the winding, two-lane highways of Vermont to my grandparents' farm on North Hero, an island in Lake Champlain. The lake was freezing cold, but we would swim anyway, and we fished a lot. One day, I caught twenty-eight perch.

Fall was my favorite time of year. The fall colors were beautiful on my street. I collected the prettiest leaves and preserved them by ironing them between two layers of wax paper. We would play hobo when it was time to burn the leaves. Huge piles of leaves would be raked into a pile. When it was time to burn them, we placed potatoes wrapped in aluminum foil in the center of the fire. We tied up our stuff in red bandanas at the end of a stick that we carried on our shoulders, and when the burning was done, we feasted on our cooked potatoes. I don't ever remember being bored. We always had so much to do.

I always thought I would grow up in Massachusetts, attend Mount Holyoke College, and always live in New England. My favorite book was Little Women, and I read it over and over. I was going to grow up to be Jo March, and I even asked my mother why she named me Ruth instead of Josephine.

When I was twelve, my grandfather passed away, and my father went to Florida to be with him before he died. My father was so taken with Florida, and it was all he talked about – the weather, no need for winter clothes, and the lower cost of living. None of us knew about his plans for our future until he came home from work in December and announced that he had given his notice at work. After the first of the year, he was leaving for Florida, and we would all follow him soon after. I was stunned. My mother was shocked. My brothers were very excited about the prospect of going to the beach every day. Shortly after his announcement, World War III broke out in our house. This was my father's decision, but my mother was angry and not at all for it. However, she was of the generation where the family was kept together at all costs. My father left for Florida, and my mother had the task of selling the house, packing everything and then driving four kids, ages seven to sixteen, to Florida in February.

In Florida, I found myself to be a fish out of water. Florida was flat, always sunny and seasonless. The schools were so behind that I was enrolled in both eighth-grade and ninth-grade classes. But in other ways, I felt lost. Just as plants mature faster in the tropics, so do the girls. I was far behind my peers, both physically and emotionally. I was still a girl in so many ways, and I knew it.

In New England, people put down roots. In Florida, the sands constantly shift, and the establishment of roots isn't fostered. Florida was booming in 1966, and the developments of ranch-style cement-block houses were mushrooming. These were not houses, streets, or towns with a history. The streets did not have names of trees, such as maple, oak, or walnut, or of people, such as Washington, Adams, or Franklin. The streets were named by letters and numbers, such as Route A1A, 22nd Street, or Third Avenue. The soft grass that we used to lie on and watch the clouds was replaced with crabgrass lawns. In New England, we killed this stuff with weed killer. I was a fair-skinned, blond girl who turned into a walking freckle from being out in the sun. I never tanned, I turned orange – freckle orange. I had landed in a distant land, and I did not fit.

But I grew to understand that a sense of place is important, and a person needs to satisfy that need in their life. Although I knew then that I would not live my life in Florida, I knew where I belonged. I eventually adjusted to life in south Florida, built some life-long relationships, and seven years later, I left. Since then, I have lived in upstate New York, the Midwest, the Mid-Atlantic, and even back in New England. And this I know for sure, in my heart's core, I am a New England Girl. I return to New England whenever I smell the salty sea air, see the crimson maple leaves in the fall, smell the wood-burning fireplaces while on a walk on a snowy winter day, or see the first crocuses in spring. Then I return to New England, and I am home.

***

After a 32-year career with the Federal Government, Ruth McCully pursued a creative life. As a personal historian, she assists people in writing their life stories through life story writing workshops based on Guided Autobiography. She is also a photographer who focuses on floral, landscape, and abstract photography.

58

A One-Way Ticket Home

by Helen Davidson

I stood on the cusp of sixty and felt old.

My mind was still sharp, my body was still fit, but I felt like I was looking at the end of the road! I could not fathom what I would do for the next ten, twenty, thirty years. My girls had started their own lives, my passion for my career had waned, and my husband and I had settled into a far-too-comfortable routine. As a life-long planner, focused on goals and achievements, I could not imagine what might feed my soul and sustain me for the coming years.

Ursula Le Guin once said, "It is good to have an end to journey toward, but it is the journey that matters, in the end." Her words resonated and made me realize that I always plan with the end in mind, paying little attention to the journey.

Instinctively, I knew these next years could be the best journey yet, but I didn't know where to start or where to go. However, I did know that to find my way, I had to step out of my comfort zone and open myself up to new experiences.

I filled my backpack with essentials, and my husband drove me to the airport for the start of a two-month solitary journey. A well-planned journey, being the planner I am, but a journey without a specific destination. A journey that I hoped would be lived day by day, built on vague memories of what used to make me happy—long walks, solitude, books, and nature—woven into new adventures designed to push my boundaries.

Travelers teemed around us as I stood in my husband's embrace at the airport. In my hand, I clutched my passport and a copy of *Wanderlust: A History of Walking* by Rebecca Solnit—the only 'real' book I would read before turning to my iPad. All I knew for sure was that I wanted to walk Santiago de Compostela—over mountains, along the ocean, down forest trails, on old Roman roads, and to places I had only dreamed of. Lewis Carroll wrote, "If you don't know where you're going, any road will take you there."

My wish, as I set out, was that walking those paths would bring me back to myself.

As I said goodbye to my husband on that blustery September morning, I held four one-way tickets in my hand.

The first ticket took me to Ovledo, Spain, the gateway to my destination, which was the village of Faedo in the Asturian Mountains. Surrounded by dramatic peaks, steep gorges, and deep valleys, I eased into my journey, stretching my muscles, re-discovering my body, and learning about the natural world around me.

Every morning I woke up before sunrise to ensure I was fueled with coffee before a ninety-minute yoga session. I would then head off with the two other guests, a couple from Belleville, Ontario, and our guide Camillo, to walk to remote villages along footpaths that had been worn down over hundreds of years. The walks were long, usually ten to fifteen kilometers, but slow, as we stopped frequently to learn about trees, plants, insects, and birds.

Halfway through the day, we stopped for meals of wild boar pâté, goat stew, and wine, which we drank from no-name bottles that were placed on the table and then measured at the end of the meal. Every night, after another ninety-minute restorative yoga session and dinner cooked from local ingredients, I would fall asleep to the sound of cowbells. My concerns about the future began to diminish, and a feeling of peace settled over me.

My second one-way ticket took me to Porto, Portugal, the gateway to the second half of the Portuguese Coastal Camino, where I started my 288-kilometer, solitary pilgrimage to Santiago de Compostela.

My pilgrimage was lonely at first. I met few travelers. Every day I was eager to get to my next hotel, knowing there would be a smiling face behind a reception desk, a hot bath, and a comfortable bed. Slowly, my sense of self began to shift. The rational part of me that always planned and organized everything to the minute began to melt away. I lived less in the planned-out future and more in the present—walking, enjoying the beauty of the world around me. My pace slowed, I took more rest stops, and I was even reluctant to stop walking as I approached my next accommodation.

My sense of time disappeared, and I lived very much in the moment. So much so in fact that one evening I completely forgot what time I was Skyping with my husband because I was deep in conversation with fellow pilgrims—yes, over a bottle of wine. My husband, worried, was about to call the hotel to see if I had arrived when my tanned, relaxed face appeared on his computer screen.

My third one-way ticket took me to Morocco. Friends were concerned that, as a western woman traveling on my own, this was not the safest destination. But I wanted to experience a culture that would test my comfort zone. I spent a few days by myself in Marrakesh and then joined an Intrepid Tour to explore southern Morocco. What I discovered was a country that filled my soul with its breathtaking beauty, kind people, and humble traditions. I spent a few nights at a homestay with a family in the Atlas Mountains. I watched the sun set and rise over the Sahara, and I ate more goat stew—which, to my surprise, I had come to love! Morocco was about suspending my beliefs and acknowledging that the world is so much richer than I had ever imagined.

My final one-way ticket was a ticket home. A journey I booked sooner than I had originally planned as, per Paulo Coelho's wise words, I could now envision a new story for my life, and I was ready to start living it.

I learned a lot about myself during this adventure, and the most important lesson was that I had to let go of planning all aspects of my life. I had to slow down and allow the journey to unfold, despite occasional discomfort. I had to trust that my life would find the right path.

This has not always been easy, as I like to plan and be in control, but this new outlook on life is working. I am discovering forgotten passions, I am being presented with interesting opportunities, and I have a renewed optimism for the future—one I am eager to explore.

***

Helen Davidson has been a writer and storyteller since childhood, recognizing early on that writing things down gives her insight and clarity. Helen is a blogger and life story facilitator, supporting women as they explore the experiences and relationships that put their lives in motion many years ago.

59

The Road Bike

by Brianne Ellsworth

L ast night I was exploring a new city. I took my Lotus road bike and hopped on a train to uncover the secrets this new place had for me to find. After meandering around, I went back to get my bike. Hundreds of bikes were whizzing by on the luggage carousel. When I saw mine and motioned to grab it, it changed colors, turning into a different bike completely. The man next to me haughtily took what turned out to be his bike. Mine was nowhere to be found. Nothing looked familiar anymore. I looked around, starting to panic. How could I not remember where I had left it? How could I lose my beloved bike?

Upon waking, I shrugged it off as another insignificant dream.

When I was twenty-three, I moved back home to Newport Beach after finishing college at San Francisco State University. I had loved living in San Francisco and how it had changed me, made me feel alive. I wasn't thrilled to be leaving, but I was eager to start an internship with a furniture designer. Settling back in my hometown proved harder than I had imagined. Sometimes I felt unrecognizable from my previous self. I felt out of place and had a hard time relating to people I'd known for most of my life. Attempting to meet new friends, I joined a vegan dining group. I mostly felt isolated and sat riddled with anxiety while trying, only sometimes successfully, to enjoy myself. The effort it took was too much. Looking for other hobbies, I decided to buy a road bike. I missed public transportation and thought relying less on my car would keep me from slipping back into suburbia.

I found a lavender and black vintage Lotus on Craigslist. As soon as I started pedaling, I knew she was mine. Unlike the beach cruisers I was accustomed to, this baby was fast. I relished the feeling of the skinny tires on the pavement and the wind in my hair. Grinning ear to ear, my sense of freedom reignited.

With my Lotus, I gripped the ideals I'd fostered in college. I rode my bike six miles each way to work. I took leisurely rides along the coast to Long Beach and to my second job as a waitress in Balboa. On days off, I rode to the library, getting lost in rows of nonfiction books. I read a memoir of a man who rode cross-country on his bike after the death of his son—a ride that sounded both grueling and exhilarating. I wanted that rush, that challenge and sense of accomplishment. I wanted to chase a big dream. I grew complacent instead, getting lost in books and romanticizing the future.

After a year of too much solitude and feeling like I didn't fit in, I became defensive when people questioned my choices. Even my dad continually cross-examined me. He couldn't understand why I valued pedaling over pumping gas or why I'd stopped eating meat. I couldn't brush it off anymore. I was tired of explaining myself. Tired of feeling alone. Tired of caring.

So I stopped. I quit my design job, worked at a restaurant, and started drinking more. It was so much easier to be social, so much easier to not care. I rode my bike to work, pretended to be happy, and drank the days away. Every day felt the same, and time seemed to stand still. Filled with apathy, I lost four years to mundane routine.

On the night of my twenty-eighth birthday, I reconnected with the man who would become my husband. Six months later, after riding our bikes on the 4th of July, I couldn't hold it in anymore and told him I loved him. We spent a lot of our time together outdoors with walks on the beach, camping, and riding our beach cruisers. Life was dreamy. I had started a vintage clothing business, volunteered to paint with seniors with dementia, and eventually left waitressing behind to manage an art program for a nonprofit. I was satisfied, though I always ached for more.

We married a few years later, and then everything slowly faded to gray. I declined social engagements for fear of bursting into tears. Avoiding reality at all costs, I often cried myself to sleep. Dreaming is impossible when you're hopeless, even when you sleep twelve hours a night.

The dissolution was so gradual that it took me fourteen months to realize that my apathy had ballooned into severe depression. My Lotus gathered dust, the tires dried and cracked. It was painful to watch her waste away and even worse to watch her permanently disappear from my life when I sold her. I hadn't wanted to, but it made sense. Why hold onto something you no longer use? Why keep a road bike when you only ever ride a beach cruiser?

I had traded in my sense of freedom and adventure for security. Falling in love, wanting children, and having a steady paycheck were positive things, so why did I resent them? Why didn't I feel satisfied? Why did I bury my dreams? What did I really want? I ventured deep into my psyche to uncover the answers, spent years focused on finding myself.

Being honest while trusting my desires and listening to my body's wisdom was a process. It still is.

When I finally opened up and shared my truth, I was met with a double-edged sword: divorce. It was both devastating and liberating. Alone, but with only one person to please: me.

In the morning, walking the dogs with my current partner, I tell him about my dream of exploring the city. Even though it feels trivial, I share it. "There's a lot to unpack in that one," he says. Bewildered, I ask for his insight. "The bike seems significant. Is it your identity?"

It hits me hard. A call to action. A warning. *Am I losing the parts of me that I've worked so hard to recover?*

Only in the dream world can you lose something that you've already lost. But in the waking world, you can find yourself again.

***

Brianne Ellsworth has been teaching Guided Autobiography to seniors since 2018. She was drawn to Guided Autobiography for its ability to bring to light stories that might not have otherwise been told. Preserved, they become a gift to those who read them.

60

I've Been Robbed

by Luann Reiter

I met Rob in a community theater production in San Diego. One of my college roommates and I had just moved to the West Coast right after graduation. Jeannie only stayed a month, but I planned to stay at least a year, and I chose local theater as a way to meet people, have fun and work together on a creative project.

Rob was handsome, kind, smart, and funny. We clicked right away and spent time at the movies, grabbing a coffee and rehearsing our lines for the play. As I got to know him better, I could feel myself becoming attracted to him. I was able to be totally myself, keeping company with him felt effortless. A few weeks later, he told me that he was coming out of the closet. Not many people knew, he was just accepting it himself.

I went through a myriad of emotions…confusion, disappointment, and despair. I remember calling my closest friend from home and talking it out, trying to make sense of it. Rob and I continued to spend time together and, as I was new to California, didn't want to lose my newfound companion. I credit him for telling me early enough that our bond could survive whatever hard feelings might have resulted.

Rob continued to work out his feelings, and I continued to listen. It was the late 1970s, and gay men were coming out of the closet in cities where they felt safe, safer than in their smaller hometown conservative communities. One such man was Tom, a friend of mine from outside the theater crowd, who was gay and open about it. My education continued one evening when Tom invited me to a local gay dive bar hidden on a small street in one of the coastal towns. Loud music pumped through the stereo system while handsome men danced, drank, and played pool with each other. The night was full of laughter and excitement, whooping and hollering and singing aloud to Donna Summer. Sitting on a stool at the bar, the expression on my face turned to awe and fascination. Who knew places like this existed? I felt as though I had been granted access to a secret society.

You see, I grew up fairly sheltered, in a time when sexual promiscuity resulted in a tarnished reputation. Even though the sexual revolution was well underway, most of the men and women that I knew weren't revolutionized…at least, as far as I knew. People kept their business to themselves. That was the mindset of my childhood.

My friendship with Rob grew as he spoke about his feelings, the gay lifestyle, and the signals gay men put out to spot others of the same attraction. He pointed things out when we were at the beach or in a restaurant – the mannerisms, the gestures, the clothing. Handkerchiefs placed in the back left pocket meant something different than the back right pocket. Where one put his key ring on his jeans meant something also. He never discussed anything specifically sexual in nature, and I didn't ask. It was intriguing and rather difficult to wrap my mind around.

I never remember thinking I could change Rob or that something was wrong with me because he wasn't attracted to me. He WAS attracted to me, just in a whole different way. Rob listened to me and asked genuine questions rather than making assumptions. What did I want out of life? "Hmmm. That's a big one." Did I want to get married? "Eventually." Have children? "Maybe." His intentional conversation allowed me to examine my own desires, goals, and dreams. Truth be told, I was young and hadn't fully cut ties with an old boyfriend back home, and I realized that I wanted to experience life before settling down.

Moving away from a tight-knit community to a low-key beach vibe was intoxicating. I felt I could breathe. A steady stream of barbecues, house parties, and beach campfires were about meeting new people and having conversations with newfound friends. One night, at the end of a party where Rob introduced me to a group of acquaintances, I could tell he was displeased with me, a rare event. "You stole my story," he said. I was confused until he explained that the first concert he attended was Herman's Hermits with the Who as the backup group, something I related that night to everyone, which prompted "oohs" and "aahs," and it was true. Once we both realized that it was true for both of us, we laughed until we cried.

It's not as though I quickly moved through a belief system steadily ingrained from my upbringing; rather, I began to look at how I felt about the beliefs. I was opening to a wider perspective through people that I met who were not like me. My worldview expanded exponentially and whether I approved or disapproved was beside the point. I met someone who had a desire that I didn't understand, yet I valued them as a person. He wasn't harming me or demanding anything of me. Why would I refuse that friendship? The more time I spent with Rob, the more I was able to look back at my theater pals in college and realize, "oh, yeah… Nick and Karl are gay." They were great guys, ones that were funny and kind and smart.

Over the years, I spent family dinners and outings with Rob's family, meeting and socializing with some of his extended family. He met his first serious boyfriend not long after we met but eventually moved on to a fresh young farm boy whom he had longed for from afar for two years. It took some time to win Jerry over, but with his endearing, consistent charm, he did.

Rob passed away from complications of AIDS in November of 1994, one month after his thirty-eighth birthday. I still miss him terribly and call upon his spirit when I need advice or comfort. His friendship opened the doorway for me to develop relationships with people who, from the outside, I appear to have nothing in common. He taught me the value of looking beyond external facades and acknowledging the person inside.

***

Luann Reiter is a teacher of Humanities with incurable wanderlust. She has taught in the United States, Asia, and the Middle East and enjoys reading, exercising, being with her dog, and spending time at the beach.

61

First Love

by Sam Uhl

I was seven when I first remember feeling intentional love. The St. Lawrence River taught me a love for nature, and the island people taught me about the best of human love.

Downie Island is home to about thirty summer cottages on the Canadian side of the famed Thousand Islands. That rock is also home to my most cherished childhood memories. Before building the cottage, my family camped on the American side at Picnic Point, Canoe Point, and Thousand Islands Park in New York. Those islands were my summer haven for seventeen years, gently shaping my character into the happy human I would become.

When my parents built a cottage, my imagination blossomed, driven by the boredom that comes with being "the baby" of the family. This ample alone time led to an insatiable curiosity about the natural world. I spent hours wandering that tree-covered granite, picking blueberries and watching wildlife. I memorized each cliff and the soggy bay that my parents owned where thousands of Trillium bloomed, seemingly at my mother's behest. Mom adored those flowers and displayed them all summer in a small vase. They made her smile with a peace reserved for the islands. Rarely did I ever see her so happy as when she was on Downie Island. I came to know a soft and light-hearted side of her on the river, so different from Nurse Betty back in Syracuse.

I explored every inch of the island, alone and with my island friends—
most of whom were my parents' age. Mr. Driesen—a senior executive
when not on the island—taught me how to filet a fish. My father bought
me a filet knife, and I felt like the most envied fisherwoman on the river
because I could catch a Great Northern Pike with a bread ball stuffed on
a single hook and prep it for a family dinner.

I loved the cool mornings, to watch the mist lifting effortlessly off the
water, vaporizing in a silent, spinning dance of worship to the rising sun.
I loved floating quietly with the engine off in that mist. Just me, my boat,
and God. It was magical to see a fish arc out of the water after some
unseen treat. In the shallows, I leaned over the gunnel to see sunshine
illuminating schools of minnows, sometimes moving zigzag and other
times suspended perfectly still, hovering above the garden of seaweed
below. They moved like one big brain. Everything under the water was
magical to me. Well, almost everything.

Some things that lurked under the water scared me, like hydro lines—
black pipes that sucked river water up to the cabins. And seaweed. I was
terrified that if my toe touched a single leaf, a muck monster would slip
out of the silt and pull me under the muck. Today I'll eat seaweed, but
I'll not be swimming with it.

I preferred the company of adults to the company of kids my age.
When I went boating alone around nearby islands (which I was entrusted
to do at the age of seven), I would drive past the noisy families playing
on the docks or swimming and head for the company of quiet people like
the remarkable Ms. Reed. She owned Potato Island, also known as
Shingwaqusie, the Native American name. It was a tiny island
surrounded closely by jagged shoals and neighboring islands.

I was frequently drawn to her dock, and by the time I tied up, she was
drifting down the path like a beautiful, rugged matriarch to greet me. I
wanted to know the secrets of such a contented, affable spirit. She was
always adorned with the gentlest, most sincere smile I'd ever seen. I
always felt welcome and loved.

Though hardy and self-sufficient, Ms. Reed had the air of noblesse about her. Her simple skirts and blouses hung comfortably on her long frame. She wore her hair in a simple bun, resting easily above her slender, elegant neck. I imagined that she must be classically trained or took etiquette lessons from the Queen. She stood tall and straight but with a gentleness that relaxed you at once. Her rough and calloused hands revealed fingernails stained with dirt. To me, this only accentuated her grace and mystery.

She moved to the island alone every spring as the ice cracked away from the mainland, and she often stayed until the first snow. She split her own wood, grew edibles and flower gardens, and drove herself everywhere in a 16-foot open boat that required her to pull-start a 25-horsepower outboard engine. Ms. Reed was reminiscent of Glinda the Good Witch from Oz coupled with the heartiness of Auntie Em. Her presence evoked safety and trust. I could tell that she'd seen things, experienced things I would never fully understand, but whose lessons would extend to me by virtue of my nearness to her.

Visits began with a simple, quiet greeting as we walked from dock to cottage, followed always by a plate of cookies and a cup of tea as we caught up on the happenings since we'd seen one another last. I'd never been served hot tea before, with the requisite offering of milk and honey or lemon. I never did take to the lemon, but the sweetness of the tea went down like an elixir that made me part of her secret realm. When her curiosity and my sweet tooth were sated, conversation intermittently continued during a stroll around the small rock that supported her cozy cottage—I could never call it a "camp," it didn't fit her nature. Her cottage was filled with books, so many that they served as the only insulation I could spot between the studs on the walls—they must have been important or classic tomes as they all looked ancient and worn with many visits to their pages. They surrounded her on high, dark wood shelves, serving as her watchmen and confidants.

She worked in winters on the mainland in the library in Gananoque, Ontario. What a natural fit for someone who believed in the sustenance of books and the sharing of their lessons with others.

The smell of her pot-belly stove gently burning the wood was magical as it warmed the room without any apparent tending. I never saw her stoke the fire or add wood. It's as though it lit itself each morning and glowed with pride to bring heat to her fine, thin bones.

Everything surrounding Ms. Reed took on the role of servants in awe and in love with their queen. She shared stories of her extensive travels to places around the world I'd never heard of. She loved those precious memories, and they kept her company in the long hours of solitude, married only to her friends and the river. I loved her deeply and still rely on the imprinted sound of her voice saying my name, full of love and acceptance—Sam, the River Rat from Downie Island.

***

Sam Uhl believes that everyone's life is a story worth telling! She helps people write their memoirs through ghostwriting, book coaching, retreats, workshops, manuscript editing, and book printing. She is the CEO & publisher at Mountain Page Press, a hybrid publishing house.

62

What. The. Fork.

by Tara Slater

*A fork in the road is a metaphor, based on a literal
expression, for a deciding moment in life or history when
a choice between presented options is required, and once
made, the choice cannot be reversed. – Wikipedia*

A nd here we are.

I can't locate anyone wearing a bright orange vest, so I'm
guessing this is up to me. I need a crossing guard. I am forty-three. I
hope to look back at this point in my life in ten years and say, "wow, girl
– you did that."

I flinch at the compliment "You are SO strong." They told me that
when I was raped in college. They told me that when I spoke at my Pop's
funeral as a teen. They told me that when I left my marriage last summer.
They say it to me now 'cause my brother suddenly died. I don't want to
be strong. I didn't ask to be strong. I want to be saved. Someone, show
me the way.

For the past four decades, I've always had the "rainbows, puppies and
kittens" positive outlook, but recently I just want to scream, pout and
shout. I've always been the firecracker. But I'm changing.

My fire is disappearing.

I'm losing my spark.

I'm on my last log.

I know I hold the match, but I'm stuck on this street, looking both ways. *Where is that damn neon orange vest?!*

So no, I'm not strong – I'm just surviving. Aren't we all?

So, which way do I go from here?

I could sob, or I could soar.

I did life backward – lived in the Florida Keys in my twenties and acted like a retiree. So now, in my forties back in my hometown, I'm stuck – now what? Life is hard, and the lessons of loss are just beginning. I'm losing friends faster than I can make new ones. My friends' babies have turned into teens, while I can hardly care for a succulent. Is this the middle of the road? Eff this fork.

So much to overcome this year. Hill after hill. Heartache. Masks. Hike. And repeat. And then, in the midst of it all, God took our Todd.

I've gotta make him proud. He is watching me – he is pressing buttons that are making me okay. So why let him see me cry and scream when I can smile, create and dream? Dream that I will see him one day, that I will talk about him to his kids all the time. I can't have him watch me wallow.

When he came to visit me in Florida one year, I brought him to our first NBA game. I stared at the celebrities on the sidelines, not really noticing the bright orange ball being tossed around on the court. Todd was in awe. I was so proud we got there. Proud, 'cause the drive there and back was SO unnecessarily long. Why? Because I was scared. I lived on an island – I didn't do highways. And to Miami? Whoa – I watched Dateline, a lot of shady stuff goes on in Miami.

But my friend had free tickets for a game that night in Miami that they wouldn't use. Would me and my brother like to go? I was in the bank, my brother waiting outside in the sunshine. I gazed at him through the bank's window while getting this offer. He'd never know if I said no. I was scared to drive to Miami. He's never gonna know if I-

"We'll go!" came out of my mouth. UGH. And so, we went.

We took the long way, but we made it.

Instead of the highway, we stayed on US1 after reaching the mainland. Sticking to the thirty-mile-an-hour back roads instead of that big, scary highway. He agreed, before we left, that I could take my own route to get us there and he would not complain. He had no idea what he was in for. Two unnecessary extra hours tossed onto our trip each way, just 'cause I didn't want to go fast.

Scaredy cat.

He was patient. I was proud. It was a great day. We got home super late after the game due to the extra hours my route tossed on. But he didn't care. We laughed, we talked, we planned. We shared memories of what it was like to grow up on Bellevue Avenue and our dreams for the next decade. It was that beautiful time when you and your sibling are finally at the age where you would choose to be friends. To this day, that will always be one of my most favorite (albeit unnecessarily long) road trips.

It's kind of hard to drive my car these days since it's just me and my thoughts, alone with the radio. I can handle my highways better now, but it's the radio that hurts. Adele hits different when your heart is broken. So, my rule when driving is, it's okay to cry behind the wheel. I walk or take the bus if it's a day I need to keep my makeup on.

The other day, driving back from visiting my nephew and niece, I was sobbing along to some dumb song when I must have looked down to glance at my phone or change the station to something less heart-piercing when I heard a voice that made me swerve.

"Are you KIDDING ME? Snap out of it!" I looked back and saw an angry woman shaking her arm at me. I must have gotten too close to her or her flower bed, but her words came clear. *Snap. Out. Of. It. Very cute, Todd. You are everywhere, huh?* – even the angry Karen in the garden wearing a muumuu.

Snap out of it. Go, drive, be. Take the long road or shortcut, but just go. No one you love wants to watch you spend your days sad, in bed. Get out there and do things.

This is the road I'll take. Slow like a turtle, but we'll get there. When your son goes to college, I'll bring him. When your daughter wants a prom dress, I'll help. When your partner has a bad day, I'll cheer her up. I can still be in the game even though you aren't. And so, once again - I'll go. Maybe slow, but I'll be strong. Nervous, but we're gonna take my route, go my way. So maybe the last half of my life is going to be like US1. It may not be the fastest, but it will be fun. We will get there.

And so now I'm left to take the long roads home without him. But I am no longer stuck since he is my guide. I'm moving. I'm rising. My log catches a spark. Maybe slow, but we go.

I can't see it yet, but under those wings, he wears an orange vest.

***

Tara Slater works at a university by day and writes by night. She enjoys meeting people, writing in calligraphy, and quoting Oprah. Before moving back to the Northeast, Tara sailed around the world working on cruise ships. She lives in Syracuse, New York.

63

Xena, Tall Trees, and Sturdy Roots

by Pamela Abbott-Enz

I have a love-hate relationship with my body. I am quite content with my appearance when I am alone in a room looking at a mirror. I have pretty great hair, my figure is proportional to my height. I can take a deep breath and not feel restricted, and most recently, I am able to wake up without joint pain.

It's when I go outside and stand next to other people that I feel bad about myself. I am either too tall or too heavy. My thighs are too big, or my breasts are too small. My crow's feet make me look old, and, my god, I look middle-aged. I'd like to kid myself that the aging thing is a surprise, but I'm very clear about the effects of turning fifty-five and what fifteen years of chronic illness and pain have done to me.

I am very conscious of my stature. I'm tall, but I'm not *tall and thin*. I'm tall and curvy. Think Xena-Warrior-Princess tall. I was often placed in the back row of school photographs because I bested many of the young boys. My curves came early. In fact, I have vivid memories of a school friend asking me why I didn't have a space between my thighs like she did. Yep, thigh gap issues at age nine. At thirteen, I got hit by the hormone fairy and was all round and squishy from then on.

Compounding the hormone whammy, I also had to contend with chronic asthma and an overprotective family. I was taught to be a sitter. As a result, I am an excellent seamstress and an avid reader, but can't ride a bike or throw a ball. I have never developed tremendous muscle strength, and my overall fitness level leaves a lot to be desired. Despite my best intentions, I continue to be "exercise averse." I have negotiated all sorts of ways to sneak exercise into my life: I park at the farthest space in the lot; I take the stairs rather than the elevator; I walk the dog. The very idea of compulsory exercise makes me twitchy. I marvel at my friends who run marathons. I firmly believe that the only time it is necessary to run is when being chased.

To get out of physical education in high school and college, I joined the marching band as a flag twirler, which unfortunately caused my lower half to become quite strong and big, rather than toned and thin. I remember bemoaning my large legs. In an attempt to cheer me up, my grandmother said, "Oh, sweetheart, don't worry. Tall trees need sturdy roots!"

My roots are still sturdy, but now I get the added benefit of varicose veins, cellulite, and "cankles." Rather than a wispy willow, I turned into an oak.

The thing that has surprised me the most about growing older is the way that injuries and illnesses came back to haunt me. In my early twenties, I was in a pretty serious car accident that caused extensive soft tissue damage. Being twenty, I hungered more for the insurance settlement than for my long-term health goals. As soon as I could, I ceased physical therapy and took the money.

Twenty-five years later, I suffer from compressed disks, a poorly healed rotator cuff, an injured neck, and both knee and wrist issues. My vocation as an online educator and my avocation as a costume designer have exacerbated these injuries. All this compounded by the bonus diagnosis of Epstein Barr Syndrome. Without proper control, I live in joint pain, muscle pain, or digestive pain. This has been pretty constant over the last fifteen years and has taken a toll on my mental health, my marriage, and certainly my appearance. It's the perfect storm for misery and apathy.

About two years ago, British stoicism was trumped by utter disgust. After going through a pretty rough patch in my marriage, I decided that I had better pay as much attention to my mind and body as I was to my relationship. I joke that it took five years of therapy, a near divorce, and a pandemic for me to spend the last year getting healthy and happy in my own skin! It was time to do some house cleaning ... and a bit of redecorating.

Taking care of me is hard work, and often feels self-indulgent. Taking the time to nurture my soul, attend to the medical requirements of my body, choose foods that do no harm, balance sleep and rest needs with my desire to be productive, and maintain my home and career is a constant challenge. Regular physical therapy, acupuncture, rest, and restructuring my diet have made a great difference. Next, I want to challenge my exercise aversion and open myself up to yoga. I do not expect to ever achieve the perfect downward dog, but I do an amazing child's pose.

So, I am in a body that I am thankful for and irritated by. Every day, I look in the mirror and try to love what I see. It's hard. I know what I want to be and struggle to get okay with where I am. I consider Botox versus bangs, and I research cosmetic surgery. I choose clothes that hide my flaws and resist the urge to buy muumuus. I have started wearing "sensible shoes" and want to cry when I see my three-inch stilettos accumulating dust, with the knowledge that wearing them will disable me for three days. I am making choices, and they often don't feel good. Letting go of my "shoulds" is hard. Learning a new set of rules is challenging as I try to be comfortable in my own skin, albeit a bit saggy, a bit heavy, and a bit lumpy.

This year I stopped coloring my hair and found myself with a surprisingly stunning silver and auburn mane. Rather than having liposuction, I have decorated my flaws with art, symbols for prosperity and images of beauty. And, every Halloween, I put on my Xena Warrior Princess costume, and I don't care what anyone thinks, even if I do have sturdy roots.

***

Dr. Pamela Abbott-Enz is a proud mother, loving wife, and professor of Gerontology. Pam has published one anthology, The Tao of Doris, *one academic textbook,* A Primer in Human Aging, *and has a blog, "Orchids and Cabbages," where she shares humor and life stories.*

64

Lesson from Beyond
by Jacqui Letran

My maternal grandmother's death created in me a sense of urgency to live fully and without regret.

When Grandma's health started to decline, no one took notice. She seemed to tire easily, started refusing invitations to gatherings, and even stopped going to her beloved temple. She went from being a talkative woman who was always busy around the house to being a woman who preferred to say very little and often hid in the comfort of her room.

Before long, Grandma started losing her short-term memory and then her long-term memory. She would forget where she was and who we were. There were occasional brief moments of clarity when Grandma would come alive, chat nonstop, and call us by our names. Then the Grandma we knew would fade away again.

I was living in the state of Washington and would fly to California to visit my family. My two sisters also lived in California. We always made it a point to stop by my uncle's house, where Grandma lived and where my two younger cousins were her caretakers. We always made sure to bring Grandma's favorite snacks of sweet sticky rice and tropical fruits, but our visits were brief.

My sisters and I have a strong dislike for our uncle and didn't enjoy being in his house, which always smelled like urine from his unruly dogs. "Besides," we would reason, "Grandma doesn't really know that we were there." After our obligatory visit, my sisters and I would spend the rest of my visit hanging out and having fun.

Grandma's health continued to go downhill. She was hospitalized for a lung infection, rapidly declined, and was transferred to hospice. Her doctors told my mother and uncle it was unlikely that Grandma would go home. Within a few days, she went into a coma.

My mother and uncle had to make the ultimate decision of whether to withdraw life support. After several days of anger and tears, they decided it was time to say goodbye.

When Grandma passed away, something in me changed. I felt so much sorrow and regret for the life Grandma had lived and how I had contributed to her pain. Like others, I had disregarded her. I was too involved in my own life to make time for sweet Grandma.

When Grandma was eighteen, she was forced to marry a man forty years older than her. Even though she had a boyfriend with whom she was madly in love, Grandma couldn't disobey her parents. She had to marry a man she did not know and did not love. From then on, her life was never hers again.

Until recently, women in my culture didn't have many rights. Women in Grandma's and even my mother's generation were raised to believe their primary jobs were to procreate and serve their husband and his family.

As much as she hated it, Grandma accepted her fate and served to the best of her abilities. Even when my grandfather passed away, Grandma remained faithful and refused to look at another man.

She continued the tradition of service and took care of my uncle's every need, regardless of how cruel he was to her. Many times, he literally dragged Grandma out into the street and told her he never wanted to see her ever again. Grandma would cry and beg for forgiveness. We pleaded with her to come live with us, but she refused. Her place was with her son, the man of the house.

Everything Grandma did was in line with the tradition of serving the man of the house. She didn't have many friends. She didn't have hobbies. She didn't have a life outside of serving my uncle.

As I reviewed Grandma's life, something clicked in me. I knew that, on my deathbed, I didn't want to look back and regret all the opportunities I didn't take. I didn't want to miss a single moment of living. I was determined to make up for all that Grandma had missed.

I started packing my calendar solid with activities. I filled every day with three to four outings with friends or solo adventures.

At first, I felt alive! I was living life and doing things Grandma could only have dreamed of.

Soon, it became too much. I would be at one event, worrying about being late to the next event. I couldn't be present to enjoy the people and activities in front of me. I was overwhelmed and exhausted, but I couldn't stop. I had made a promise to myself to live fully, not just for me, but for Grandma. I had to honor my promise.

Months later, I visited Thailand, land of the many Buddha statues. As I was climbing the steep and strenuous 1,260 steps to reach the summit of Tiger Cave Temple, I thought of Grandma. Although she didn't have many interests and hobbies, she would have loved to see the many Buddha statues here. I wished I'd had the foresight to take Grandma to Thailand when she was alive.

Instantly, I felt Grandma's presence and knew she was with me. I had a heavy backpack on me that day, and I imagined it was Grandma that I was carrying. I took my time, looking at everything slowly, making sure Grandma had enough time to enjoy the beauty and splendor of it all. I felt connected to Grandma like I had never felt before and felt a huge burden being lifted.

Grandma had forgiven me, and I had forgiven myself. I didn't realize how much guilt I was carrying for not appreciating Grandma when she was alive. I had so much guilt for not showing Grandma the love and care she deserved. I cried silently, not because I was sad, but because I had finally found peace.

After that trip, I stopped over-committing and slowed down. Grandma was not an educated woman but taught me to stop taking things for granted. She taught me to be present and live my life with intention and love. This is the lesson I chose to honor for the rest of my time on earth.

***

Jacqui Letran is a nurse practitioner, author, speaker, and teen confidence expert. With more than twenty years of experience working with teens in medical and holistic settings, she provides time-tested, practical guidance to help teen girls embody Peaceful Confidence™. Her multi-award-winning book series Words of Wisdom for Teens *is considered a go-to resource for teens, parents of teens, and anyone working with teens.*

Ready to Write Your Story?

Learn how to write your life stories and connect with other life story writers by joining a Guided Autobiography program in your neighborhood or online.

Our instructors and their classes are listed online at:
www.GuidedAutobiography.com

Acknowledgments

This first Birren Center collection is only possible thanks to the collaborative spirit of the GAB Family.

Special thanks to the publication team – Cheryl Svensson, the heart of GAB; Peggy Rosen, the sunshine; Val Perry, the voice of reason; Robin Brooks, the eye of design; Jacqui Letran, the self-publishing whisperer; and Sarah White, the marketing elf.

Much gratitude goes to the volunteer readers and proofreaders who got the first peek and gave their editorial feedback – Christy Lyons, Marilyn Hayat, Patricia ONeill, Rachael Wurtman, Kristi Cromwell, Charity Crabtree Van Dyck, Talula Cartwright, Helen Davidson, Luann Reiter, Brianna Madden, Pam Toal, Katrina Anderson, Lori Stokan Smith, Mimi Holmes, Pat McNees, Sarah White, Richard Campbell, Veronica Laboure Slaughter, Joanne Mujic, Sheila Spencer, Michele Halseide, Philip Holden, Micki Sauer, and Tisha Martin.

Thank you to all of the instructors who do the amazing work of helping people heal their hearts as they write their stories. And thank you to all who submitted their work, wearing tender hearts on sleeves in order that their stories might be shared with others. Whether or not your words made it into these pages, the world is enriched by your bravery and vulnerability.

Finally, thank you to Cheryl Svensson, who answered her phone, listened to my idea, and gave her blessing on one condition – "Please don't do this alone." Without her, and the team that followed, and the GAB community who submitted their stories and cheered us on every step of the way, this book would have been even more humble.

About the Editor

Emma Fulenwider calls herself "the Lifestorian" because she's on a mission to help a million people save their life stories.

A former ghostwriter turned memoir coach, she believes that autobiographical writing is a peace-making practice because it invites us to compassionately connect with ourselves and with others.

In 2015, at a conference for the Association of Personal Historians, Emma attended Cheryl Svensson's seminar on Guided Autobiography and was awed by GAB's ability to offer healing in a hurting world. In 2019, she completed her instructor training and now supports Cheryl and the GAB community as editor of the Birren Center's publishing team.

Emma lives in Sacramento, where she conspires with her husband, Thomas, to raise arguably the two goofiest children on earth.